TODAY'S LONDON BUSES

Front Cover: The 8 for some time had a shared allocation with Willesden Garage where it terminated but that garage lost it in 1992, when the route was withdrawn between Willesden Garage and Bond Street where it was diverted over the withdrawn 25 routing to Victoria. Here we see the 'New Routemaster', or LT as they have been classed, crossing the impressive Holborn Viaduct which passes above Farringdon Street. LT462 (BW) is allocated to Bow where this route has managed to be retained during retendering for many years. Sunday 21 October 2018.

Title Page: The 390 was Metroline's second route converted back to crew operation back in December 2013, nine years after it previously lost its crew buses back in September 2004. This route was introduced in 2003 between Archway and Marble Arch, replacing the section of route 10 between King's Cross and Archway when that route was curtailed and converted to OPO and won on tender to another operator. In late 2004, it was extended to Notting Hill Gate to cover the withdrawal of the 12. For a brief period, as a result of major road works, the route served a temporary terminus at Lancaster Gate Station but was later reinstated back to Notting Hill Gate. The route has been diverted to terminate at Victoria since 2017, where it has replaced the 73 which only goes as far as Oxford Circus now. LT117 (HT) rounds Marble Arch with its conductor visible at the back. Tuesday 3 March 2015. (*Graham Smith*)

TODAY'S LONDON
BUSES

Reiss O'Neill

PEN & SWORD
TRANSPORT

AN IMPRINT OF PEN & SWORD BOOKS LTD.
YORKSHIRE – PHILADELPHIA

First published in Great Britain in 2021 by
PEN & SWORD TRANSPORT
An imprint of
Pen & Sword Books Ltd
Yorkshire - Philadelphia

Copyright © Reiss O'Neill, 2021

ISBN 978 1 47382 104 0

The right of Reiss O'Neill to be identified as author of this work has been asserted by him in accordance with the Copyright, Designs and Patents Act 1988.

A CIP catalogue record for this book is available from the British Library.

Typeset by SJmagic DESIGN SERVICES, India.
Printed and bound in India by Replika Press Pvt. Ltd.

Pen & Sword Books Ltd incorporates the Imprints of Pen & Sword Books Archaeology, Atlas, Aviation, Battleground, Discovery, Family History, History, Maritime, Military, Naval, Politics, Railways, Select, Transport, True Crime, Fiction, Frontline Books, Leo Cooper, Praetorian Press, Seaforth Publishing, Wharncliffe and White Owl.

For a complete list of Pen & Sword titles please contact

PEN & SWORD BOOKS LIMITED
47 Church Street, Barnsley, South Yorkshire, S70 2AS, England
E-mail: enquiries@pen-and-sword.co.uk
Website: www.pen-and-sword.co.uk

or

PEN AND SWORD BOOKS
1950 Lawrence Rd, Havertown, PA 19083, USA
E-mail: Uspen-and-sword@casematepublishers.com
Website: www.penandswordbooks.com

Contents

Acknowledgements

I would like to thank the following people for their help, time, and patience over the past year: John Scott-Morgan, Terry Wong Min, Jimmy Sheng, Graham Smith, and Jim Blake, some of whom have allowed me to use some of their photographs in this book – I am truly grateful for the help you have given. I would like to thank Janet Brookes and her team for being patient with me and helping to make sure there are no mistakes in the text.

Introduction

London's Buses – The Last Eleven Years.

London has always been a very special and unique city of the world and it is only right that it should have a transport system to match that status. London's first Underground railway opened on 10 January 1863 between Farringdon Street and Paddington, but what always seems to be overshadowed is the fact that London had its first bus service operating some 34 years beforehand.

London's First Omnibus and the London General Omnibus Company (LGOC)

On 4 July 1829, a coachbuilder and stable keeper by the name of George Shillibeer started the first omnibus service in the capital. He named his bus service Omnibus, with the route following much of today's route 205 between Paddington along the Marylebone Road (then called 'New Road'), Somers Town, and City Road before terminating at The Bank. The service was well patronised but competition from other 'Pirate' companies led George Shillibeer into bankruptcy. The 'pirate' companies would continue vying for custom well into motor bus days before the formation of the London Passenger Transport Board in 1933.

The London General Omnibus Company (LGOC) you could say (apart from George Shillibeer's short operation) was London's first principal bus operator, being established in 1855. This bus company lasted right the way through until its incorporation into the London Passenger Transport Board (LPTB) in 1933 and, unlike poor George Shillibeer, survived the 'pirate' operators who competed to steal other operators' passengers. The LGOC very smartly bought out hundreds of independent operators and absorbed the routes and vehicles into its company, in order to amalgamate and regulate the many private horse bus and omnibus services that were competing against it, making it the largest omnibus operator in London at the time, controlling 600 out of the 810 omnibuses operating at the time on London's streets.

The LGOC began using motorbuses in 1902 and became a manufacturer of its own purpose-built bus, the famous B Type, the first entering service in 1910. The introduction of the B Type spelled the end for horse bus operation with its last horse bus departing London Bridge Station on Service 32 on the 25 October 1911. Thomas Tilling, another reputable London bus operator of the time, would operate London's last ever horse omnibus on 4 August 1914 between Peckham and Honor Oak Tavern, interestingly the date that the First World War was declared (perhaps the horses were commandeered for war use). The LGOC's successor, London Transport, would similarly absorb independent operators into one operating body under the Act of Parliament and would also design and build its own buses purposely for London.

The B Type bus would be the first of London's specially designed standardised buses for London, and was mass built in large quantities by the LGOC. The first entered service in 1910 gradually replacing the company's horse buses and by December 1913, the fleet had reached 2,500 vehicles and were very reliable machines revolutionising bus travel in London at the time. They were so reliable that four years after being introduced, they would be sent to the Western Front during the First World War, where they would carry troops and wounded often 'crewed' by the bus drivers and conductors who were working on them in London when they were conscripted. Here, at the Routemaster 60 event in Finsbury Park, we see recently beautifully restored B2737 belonging to the London Transport Museum. Saturday 12 July 2014.

First World War

During the First World War, a great number of London's bus drivers and conductors were called up to serve in the trenches on the Western Front. Due to their driving experience, many would be given driving posts to help with troop movements, using much of London's bus fleet, some converted into army style trucks, but a large number appearing as normal London buses freshly commandeered from service until they could get converted. It is sadly a well-known fact that many did not return from the Western Front but those who did were hugely decorated with medals of bravery and took part in the yearly remembrance parades that took place, with many returning back to their driving and conductor roles. The First World War would also be London's first flirtation with women working on the buses as clippies, cleaners, and engineers only, as they were not permitted to drive.

London Passenger Transport Board (LPTB)

The London Passenger Transport Act was passed by parliament in 1931, whereby all private bus companies and Underground Railways would be amalgamated under one governing body in the public sector. On 1 July 1933, the London Passenger Transport Board came into effect, inheriting some very antiquated vehicles and rolling stock as well as some newly built ones that would become design classics. It would also inherit some bus routes which today would be classed as outer London routes into the country area which became known as London Country. However, before the coming of the Greater London Council in 1965, whereby the London area had been downsized, many of the operating areas of some routes were still within the London area. The LPTB would become known simply as London Transport to staff and Londoners alike. London Transport would bring about the development of a clean and modern transport network which would become the envy of the world, thanks to the Chairman Lord Ashfield and Vice Chairman Frank Pick (who even got medals for architecture from Adolf Hitler and Stalin for Underground station architecture of the 1930s and '40s) pushing it into what would be called and viewed as LT's golden years.

Everything from staff cutlery, stationery and uniforms, to vehicles and even bus stop flags, shelters, and street furniture would be carefully designed and thought through so that it would be long lasting and fit for purpose, and ensuring that everything was standardised into a corporate being instead of having everything mixed and different.

Trams, Trolleybuses, And Motor Buses

The LPTB had inherited some very old vehicles when it took over the major tramway companies as well as the private municipals such as London United Tramways and Metropolitan Electric Tramways, and the LGOC's fleet. Bit by bit, LT started to replace the older vehicles it had inherited with specially designed modern vehicles with classics such as the STL, RT, RM, and RF to name some of the more known ones, although it did inherit a few new designs from the LGOC era such as the ST and LT type buses which had developed greatly since its B Type buses.

London's first experimental tram route was introduced a short route along Victoria Street in 1857 by the LGOC. However, due to parliamentary opposition, its proposed tramway would be dropped. After several other unsuccessful experiments, London finally got its first three short routes in 1870 pulled along by horses. Towards the end of the century, these tramways would gradually upgrade to electric power, offering a fast and cheap method of transport for Londoners competing with the steam railways and the new motor buses. The last tram routes were withdrawn in 1952. Here, at the London Trolleybus 50 event, we see an example of the trams that lasted until the end standing next to A1 class trolleybus 'Diddler' No.1 which was introduced in 1931, replacing the trams out of Fulwell Depot. The design of this class of trolleybus resembled a motor bus in many respects but later classes to come would be of a more modern, futuristic design. Sunday 6 May 2012.

It would inherit London United's Trolleybus system in South West London and gradually favour this silent, trackless mode of electric transport, replacing much of its tramway network with trolleybuses especially in North, East and West London. A few tram routes would survive however due to the intervention of the Second World War, after which LT decided that they would rather replace the last remaining trams and entire Trolleybus network with motor buses. London's last trams ran on 5 July 1952, with the last trolleybus following ten years later on 8 May 1962. It has of course come full circle again with the introduction of the Croydon Tramlink, but this hasn't expanded to other parts of London, although proposals have come and gone over the years. Perhaps clean, pollution-free trolleybuses may return?

Second World War

In 1939, LT had just started building and introducing its latest design of bus into service that would aim to standardise its fleet – the RT – when another war was declared, allowing only RT1 to enter service. RT2-151 were delivered between autumn 1941 and early 1942 in dribs and drabs, with production resuming in 1947. Like during the First World War, many employees would be called up or answer the call to serve, but due to a new type of warfare many drivers would be kept behind in London to continue driving as a reserved occupation as part of the Home Front war effort. Women would once again return as clippies, and in various engineering roles which required muscle work, but still they were not allowed to drive the bus.

Staff who fought returned and were decorated with their respective medals, with many returning to their driving, conductor, and engineering jobs. But LT would decide to change its policy slightly and allow women to become conductors, with many taking up the position in the late 1940s, but only if they were unmarried and didn't have children.

Recruitment 1950s and 1960s

The 1950s would see London Transport with a staff shortage problem. London Transport would start a recruitment drive in other parts of the country such as Scotland, Northern England and eventually in Ireland, with many applying and getting the job, but this was not enough to ease the shortages; so in 1956, at the request of the Barbados government, London Transport travelled to the Caribbean to recruit men and women directly from Barbados to come to work as bus drivers/conductors, Underground staff, and canteen assistants. This recruitment would last until 1970 with recruitment spreading to Jamaica and Trinidad in 1966, although many who migrated before this recruitment drive had already joined LT. London Transport would see a further influx of migrant workers from other Commonwealth countries in Africa and Asia. My grandfather came from Barbados and would be one of those bus drivers at Barking Garage in East London.

The Routemaster and RT

The famous Routemaster bus would be London's last bus that was designed especially for London service and built in London by Londoners. The bus was designed to replace the trolleybus fleet that was gathering pace in the latter half of the 1950s into the early 1960s, and would latterly be used to replace some of the RT family. Ironically, although the Routemaster did replace some of the RT family of vehicles, they did in fact operate side by side longer than was anticipated until the last day of RT operation on 7 April 1979. The Routemaster was far advanced for its time, having power assisted steering for the driver, suspension, and interior saloon heating for the passengers. The bus served Londoners for many decades and outlived a great many bus types built to replace it, but the day came that all enthusiasts dreaded; on Friday 9 December 2005, the last ever crew operated Routemaster operated in normal passenger service on Brixton Garage's route 159.

Heritage Routes 9H and 15H

Two heritage routes were created using twenty Marshall refurbished Routemasters with hopper windows and Dennis Dart engines on parts of routes 15 (Tower Hill to Trafalgar Square) and 9 (Aldwych to Royal Albert Hall) running every 15 minutes. The 9H would later be cut back to Trafalgar Square and extended to Kensington High Street at a 20-minute interval and later withdrawn altogether, with the 15H cut to a 20-minute interval also. The 15H now only runs weekends and Bank Holidays between March and October.

The Decline

The 1960s would see the decline of London Transport from its golden years. The long 1958 bus strike saw routes being withdrawn and many passengers lost to car patronage. With this came more cars on the road, in turn causing the well-known problem of today, Traffic! Traffic problems would see the once long cross London routes operating in sections, split, or withdrawn completely which is not appealing to would be passengers. On 1 January 1970, the country area routes and vehicles from London Transport were absorbed into the newly created National Bus Company, leaving LT in charge of the Red Central area services and NBC in charge of the Country area and Green Line routes. LT were now buying 'off the peg' buses that were not suitable for London conditions, frequently breaking down, also suffering spare parts shortages with some vehicles being off the road for more of their service life than in service, but this was a blessing in disguise as it kept the trusty reliable RT, RM, and RF family buses in service for longer than they should have been.

After the last RT and RF buses were withdrawn in 1979, the 1980s would see the turn of the Routemaster to start being withdrawn, with many being bought by bus operators outside London such as Glasgow, Southend and Blackpool to name a few, to use in the new tendering regime brought about by privatisation. Thankfully, Routemasters would survive privatisation of London's bus routes and continue to be an advantage with its driver and conductor over the one person operated buses into the 2000s.

One of the more successful OPO 'off the peg' types to operate in London service was the MCW Metrobus, with the first entering service in 1978, replacing the unreliable DMS, as well as the trusty RT and Routemasters in some instances. Here, at Lakeside, we see M1 which was one of the first three experimental vehicles that entered trial service at Cricklewood Garage on route 16. The trial was obviously very successful as London Transport would go on to operate more than 1,400 vehicles with the last examples bowing out in 2004. Here, M1 loads up at Lakeside on the Ensignbus annual running day; after serving in front line service for many years this vehicle was kept by Metroline in its private hire fleet before finally being preserved by Ensignbus, who thankfully use it on many occasions and special running days. Saturday 1 December 2018.

Chiswick Works and Aldenham Overhaul Works

Chiswick Works dated back to LGOC days and was where some of its buses were built. It would later become a chassis overhaul workshop as well as the training centre for London's novice bus drivers. Chiswick passed out the best drivers in the land with its skid pan to teach drivers to control the bus in wet and icy conditions.

Aldenham was originally to be an Underground Depot on the Northern Line extension over the Northern Heights to Bushey Heath but eventually, after much politics, it was not to be and instead the building was set up as an overhaul works, and would be used during the Second World War to construct aircraft and other vehicles. Due to LT designing and building its buses like a Meccano kit, this meant that it was easier to fix and replace worn and damaged components and parts. Aldenham was set up

After a couple of vehicle fires when introduced, the bendy bus fleet settled down on routes 12, 18, 25, 29/N29, 38/N38, 73/N73, 149, 207, 436, 453/N453, and Red Arrow routes 507 and 521 until the last were withdrawn from route 207 on 9 December 2011. An example is depicted here of East London's 23032 (RM) opposite Mile End Station. The bendy buses necessitated roadside ticket machines as you could not pay cash on board to the driver, you had to use an Oyster card, or passengers could purchase a batch of tickets from the newsagents that they would tear off and hand to the driver upon entry, also indicated by yellow bus stop number E plates. When Stagecoach London sold its London operations to Macquarie Bank, the old LT operating districts and logos were reintroduced, bringing back the names of East London and Selkent. Stagecoach finally bought back its London Operations and in 2020 will be operating route 25 again after winning the tender from Tower Transit. Monday 13 September 2010.

in a very organised manner, with sections of the workshop each fixing certain parts. The bus would go around in a production line system, with each part being taken off, fixed, then put back into its respective position with the bus then moving to the next section. The results would be astonishing with, for example, a 15-year-old RT bus leaving after overhaul looking, smelling and behaving like a brand-new bus off the production line. Sadly, politics, privatisation and the moving of repair work to local bus garages saw Aldenham sold off to investors to build an industrial estate and retail complex.

Vehicle Types

From the bus's humble beginnings in the nineteenth century, the vehicle types and design are very important. Each route up to the current day would have a certain vehicle allocation tailored to suit the needs, demand and patronage of that individual route. From the building of the B Type right up until the Routemaster, which would be the last bus designed and built specially for London service and road conditions, a lot of thought and testing went into the design, along with the overhaul system which LT carried out to see that vehicles have a very long life span, and vehicles up to 40 years old could look and perform as good as new. London Transport would still have some input with design and specification with some of the 'off the peg' buses it purchased; 2012 would see for the first time in decades a bus designed specifically for London service with the intention of reintroducing 'conductors' by then Mayor Boris Johnson, when the New Bus for London later classed as LT was unveiled to the public. These buses have three sets of doors just like the bendy buses which had been replaced the previous year in December 2011, have a back door which could be locked open so the bus can operate in crew mode. The first 'Crew' route was introduced in 2013 but this concept would not last long, with all the 'conductors' being made redundant in 2016 as part of cuts within the TfL empire. With the introduction of the Low Emissions Zone (LEZ) within the London area, we are seeing the whole of Central London having to be operated by Hybrid Diesel/Electric vehicles. This has seen older diesel engine vehicles pushed out to the suburbs or replaced by slightly newer vehicles; these too will probably be replaced by new Hybrid vehicles sooner or later.

Privitisation, Tendering, and the Future

Privatisation, it could be argued, has its advantages but from many passenger and staff perspectives it could be a scourge. London Transport was required to tender out bus routes from 1985 and this would later cause garage closures which would later be sold off to private investors for the land. This could also be said to be the point that London's transport started to be treated as a business instead of an important service to Londoners. Tendering sees some routes and vehicle types changing frequently from company to company at the end of their operating contract. The future of London's bus network in 2019 is looking slightly bleak with further government funding cuts meaning less money to invest and only relying on fares and sponsorships to generate spending revenue. Although we are seeing a bigger fleet of greener, more environmentally friendly Hybrid buses being introduced and a hopper fare under the current mayor to travel on as many buses as you like within the hour, we are seeing long time routes being culled back more and more to the point of it not being a use to the passenger. There are also the plans to slash many of the Central London area routes which are the artery of some passengers' travel, terminating them short of the traffic objective, which is going to deter patronage instead of encourage it, when you may have to take two or three buses instead of the one to do your original journey or forced to use the Underground. We can only sit and wait to see which changes go ahead, and in time maybe we will see a Lord Ashfield and Frank Pick of the twenty-first century return London's transport network to its former glory days that the fare paying passengers deserve. I would just like to state that some historical and general facts have been used in the text, but this book is not and does not intend to be a definitive history about London's buses. Some of the information and plans that are discussed in this book at the time of writing are current but of course, as with many things, decisions get changed over time or last minute so what may have been planned at the time of writing could have changed at the time of printing, and get interpreted as wrong information. I have also tried my hardest to research and go back through my logs of events so that correct dates and places are stated, but should you find any that are wrong please do feel free to inform us so that we can correct it for any reprints that may take place.

Reiss O' Neill.

Chapter 1

Stagecoach

A quiet morning sees TA1 (T) picking up in Oxford Street, the first of many differing batches of Low Floor Dennis Tridents purchased by Stagecoach London to oust its remaining Leyland Titans and still almost new Volvo Olympians. By the late 2000s, these early batches of Tridents were starting to get withdrawn from their remaining garages at Barking and Upton Park. TA1 soldiered on at Leyton Garage on the 55 where it was well looked after. Route 55 was chosen to trial crew operation again but using some later build Dennis Tridents in 2000; this did not last very long, however, with the route converting back to OPO not long afterwards. Saturday 31 May 2008.

Started in the 1980s, the Docklands and Beckton areas have seen change and development dramatically beyond all recognition. At Gallions Reach DLR station, Plaxton Pointer Dart 34349 (BK) picks up a couple of passengers having just started its circuitous journey to Redbridge, Falmouth Gardens. This route started as a Docklands Minibus route using Mercedes Benz minibuses in their attractive blue and white livery. Over time, the route has seen an extension from Beckton Savacentre (now Sainsburys) to Beckton Asda where it serves a bus station that was newly built to replace a smaller one. This route has also seen some re-routings in recent times; instead of serving Longbridge Road and turning into South Park Drive passing its home garage, it now serves Ilford Lane turning into Loxford Lane before it gains the routing on South Park Drive, as well as a special road built between Showcase Cinema and Barking Road alongside the A13. Sunday 21 September 2008.

19

In February 2009, Stagecoach route 276 gained some hybrid Optare Tempo's but when that route was lost to Go-Ahead in 2011, the hybrid buses made spare were transferred over to route 380 at Catford Garage. 25112 (TL) is seen in Blackheath with a row of Georgian Buildings some of which form part of the Clarendon Hotel as its backdrop. Note the vehicle's cherished RM registration plate, WLT 461, that was once worn by RM461, that was allocated to Camberwell Garage. Tuesday 23 April 2013. (*Terry Wong Min*)

This Catford Garage E200 was treated to a special red and grey Selkent livery from the early 1990s and given what is known as the 'Eyes Down' moquette which was introduced by London Buses on most buses of the 1990s, including refurbished Routemasters. This was accompanied by E400 10136, also seen in this chapter, and both were specially painted during the 'Year of the Bus' in 2014, in conjunction with Catford Garage open day. 36343 [TL) is seen passing through the picturesque Dulwich Village on its way to Lewisham. The P4 has always been a single deck route from its inception in 1972 starting with the FS 'Ice Cream Vans', then it received BLs which in turn were replaced by Leyland Nationals. The Nationals lasted until 1991 when the route was won on tender by Stagecoach using Wright bodied Darts dubbed the modern RF due to its similar split windscreen. Monday 14 April 2014. (*Terry Wong Min*)

On the other side of the large Blackheath we see Catford's 12266 (TL) which unusually has its fleet number positioned on the front left-hand side corner instead of in the middle beneath the windscreen. Blackheath sits in both the Royal Borough of Greenwich and the London Borough of Lewisham. There is an urban myth that Blackheath is a big grave site from the Great Plague of 1665 where mass burials from the thousands who died took place here although it has never officially been proven. Saturday 3 May 2014. (*Terry Wong Min*)

The 'Year of the Bus' in 2014 saw several special events held throughout the year with garage open days at some garages that had never held one before. Other events to which we were treated for the first time in many years included a few vehicles repainted into special liveries of early operators. Catford Garage held an open day on 10 May 2014 and, as part of the celebrations, it painted one of its E400 10136 in this attractive early London Transport livery and named it 'Selkent Ambassador', reupholstering its seat covers in the orange, brown and black seat moquette carried by Leyland Titans, Metrobuses, and London Underground Rolling stock which entered service in the 1980s. Here it is in Walworth Road, having just left its newly extended terminus at Elephant & Castle. Leyland Olympian L136 also received this livery in 1991 celebrating 100 years of Lewisham's first trams. Saturday 27 September 2014.

Introduced on 23 January 1999 between North Greenwich Station and Thamesmead, the 472 replaced two routes in the process, the 272 and X72. At the time, both the Jubilee Line extension and the Millennium Dome were in the process of being completed and a new bus station was incorporated into the new Underground station to help improve connections from South East London to other parts of the capital. This route was operated by some of the short-lived step entrance Volvo Olympian VN class before they were ousted by Low Floor Dennis Tridents in 2000. It has been allocated to Plumstead Garage from its conception and here we see 12346 (PD) pulling out the bus station for Thamesmead. Thursday 7 November 2014.

On a wet and dismal night of 27 April 1960, Walthamstow Trolleybus Depot's route 625 operating between Woodford and Winchmore Hill was withdrawn, with the depot becoming Walthamstow Bus Garage the very next day. The new Routemaster bus would replace the clean and silent trolleybuses here and route 275 would be one of the new routes. The route still serves the Walthamstow and Woodford areas to this day, just as the former trolleybus route did; Leyton's 10182 (T) departs the stop outside Waltham Forest Town Hall in this all-over Stagecoach Megabus advert. This is one of several adverts Stagecoach has adorned on some chosen vehicles in recent years often adding a touch of colour and brightness to the usual all-over red. Saturday 8 November 2014.

Bromley Garage is one of the less talked about garages in Stagecoach London's empire, sitting in the south eastern corner of its operating area. One of the routes allocated to it is the 61 which serves today between Bromley North Station and Chislehurst, which has kept the charm of a country village. Both Bromley and Chislehurst were historic towns in the County of Kent. 19134 (TB) is a longer version of the E400 built by Alexander Dennis; many of these vehicles have now been converted to open top and used on the Megabus Sightseeing Tour routes replacing Dennis Tridents. Saturday 19 September 2015. (Jimmy Sheng)

5 May 2018 saw Stagecoach take over the operation of route 474 from Go-Ahead Docklands Buses, where it has been allocated to West Ham Garage. Here we see one of the new buses ordered for the route 19858 (WH) at West Silvertown DLR Station. A new route to the Beckton and North Woolwich area introduced in 1999, operated by Blue Triangle between Canning Town, Hermit Road and East Beckton Asda follows a circuitous route via London City Airport, Silvertown, and North Woolwich. This was a very interesting route at the time as one could often find Leyland Titans and Metrobuses operating the route before it was converted to low floor operation with East Lancs bodied Dennis Tridents and Scania Omnidekkers. This route subsequently saw an extension from Beckton Bus Station to Manor Park paralleling routes 101 and 104. Saturday 5 May 2018.

The 473 was newly introduced between Stratford and North Woolwich on 25 September 1993, replacing parts of route 173 between Stratford and the Greengate, and part of the 276 between the Greengate and London City Airport, being tendered to the well-known company Grey Green. Stagecoach held onto the route along with sister route 262 successfully for just over two decades before both were won by Tower Transit. The year before the route was lost sees 15075 (WH) heading for Stratford as it approaches London City Airport. Buses in both directions serve the airport in the same direction driving alongside this bridge structure which carries the DLR to a station serving the airport. Most of these Scania buses have come off lease now with some ending up with Sullivan Buses. Saturday 5 May 2018.

Route 330 originally operated between Blackwall Station and Wanstead Park Station using Plaxton Pointer Darts when introduced in 1993 but was cut back to Canning Town Station in 1999. This route was then converted to double deck Scania's the route to this day has held onto its upper deck, for which the passengers of the busy Green Street and Canning Town Station are probably grateful. The hot 2018 summer sees the old order 18263 (WH) nearing journeys end on the Barking Road, but the Tridents' presence on the route would soon be coming to an end when the MMCs took over. Saturday 5 May 2019.

It is hard to believe from the settings in this picture that 10102 (WH) in Forest Drive, Manor Park is minutes away from the busy Romford Road. This route number moved into the East London area in 1989, using Leyland Titans out of the now demolished Upton Park Garage and is a route I remember using regularly, having grown up in East Ham. This route is planned to be diverted away from East Ham High Street and Manor Park to terminate at Beckton Bus Station, with a new proposed 304 route that would run from Custom House where it would travel down Prince Regent Lane, through Newham Hospital to Lonsdale Avenue taking over the 104s current routing to Manor Park. Saturday 5 May 2018.

Long established route 53 once provided a cross London connection between north and south of the River Thames. It would be hard for some people today to believe that in August 1969, this route had an allocation of 49 buses Monday to Friday. The 1970s and 80s saw this route operating between Camden Town and Plumstead Station and was one of the routes to have a brief flirtation with the Metropolitan Scania MD class between 1977-81, it would later regain its Routemasters before they were permanently withdrawn on 16 January 1988. In 1984 the route was extended from Camden Town up to Parliament Hill fields replacing that section of route 3 but this would later be cut to Oxford Circus. Plumstead's 12383 (PD) passes Westminster Station, this route has since been cut back to terminate at County Hall. Sunday 3 June 2018.

Before 1970, the 86 plied between Limehouse and Upminster Station/Upminster Park Estate and had an allocation at Hornchurch, Seven Kings, Upton Park, the original West Ham in 1982, and even Forest Gate Garages, all of which are now closed and long demolished. The route would be cut back to its current form in 1991 where it would only serve between Stratford and Romford. After the rebuilding of Seven Kings Garage was completed in 1976, Routemasters ruled supreme until they were replaced by crew operated Leyland Titans in 1984. In 2018 three types were seen operating side by side, the last remaining Dennis Tridents, E400s, and the latest version of E400 MMC as depicted here, North Street garages 10301 (NS) 'Martyn Henderson' picks up at the Wangey Road stop in Chadwell Heath with this special advert for Macmillan Cancer. Saturday 20 July 2018.

The 247 fell into the routes chosen for TfL's route branding scheme in the Romford, Ilford and Barking areas. Here we see North Street 17979 (NS) hurrying down Collier Row Lane on its way into Romford. This bus was the last survivor of the short wheelbase version of the Dennis Trident in the garage and was the only bus on the route with its full route branding. This route used to venture into the Essex countryside to Brentwood at its eastern end, and until 1993 served Ilford until it was curtailed at Barkingside. Saturday 29 September 2018.

A direct trolleybus replacement route for the 691 trolleybus on the 19 August 1959, most of the conversions in 1959 used RT buses. The route was allocated to Seven Kings and Barking Garages. Today's route operates between Clayhall, The Glade and Barking. The route saw a small share of RMs on Saturdays between 1964 and 1970 before the RT returned again until conversion to the DMS in 1973. The 169 had three offshoot routes, the 169A/B/C, all of which differed and served differing termini from the parent route. This route holds a special place in my heart as it is the main route that my grandad drove out of Barking garage. Here we see 19775 (BK) at Barkingside Station. Saturday 29 September 2018.

August 2019 saw the withdrawal of the last remaining Dennis Tridents with Stagecoach London. The last few held on at Plumstead on the 472 and at Leyton on the 215 with the odd sightings some days on the 275. In the last weeks, only two survived; 17811 (T) and the other, 17836 (T), seen here turning out of Walthamstow Central Bus Station. Lee Valley Campsite is sited alongside King George's Reservoir, stretching between Enfield Lock and Ponders End, and once the route passes Chingford Mount the scenery becomes more outer suburbs before the last stretch of route passes fields and woodlands. 17811 (T) had the honour of being the last Dennis Trident in service on 19 August 2019. Friday 9 August 2019.

On 7 July 2005 London experienced the devastation of a terrorist attack when four bombs detonated on its public transport system, three on the Underground, and one on a bus operating on route 30 at Tavistock Square killing and injuring many. As a mark of remembrance to those that were injured or lost their lives, and to replace the damaged bus, a new Dennis Trident built with a slightly longer E400 body was built and given the name *Spirit of London*. In September 2019, 19000 *Spirit of London* (RM) is based at Rainham Garage and is seen at Roneo Corner, Romford working the 252 to Hornchurch Town Centre. It was originally delivered with a dot matrix blind, but a few years after entering service it received the conventional style blinds. Friday 13 September 2019.

Route 47 used to be a long route between Farnborough and Shoreditch. In 1961, it was extended from Shoreditch to Stoke Newington as part of the trolleybus replacement program in stage 11, with a further extension to Stamford Hill between January 1965 and January 1970. Today, it terminates at Shoreditch and gets no further south than Bellingham, where it terminates at its home garage of Catford. 13100 (TL) is in Shoreditch High Street, having replaced the earlier E400s which in turn replaced Dennis Tridents. Friday 21 September 2019

Recently won on tender from Arriva, the 128 has just joined the ranks at North Street Garage. Most of the buses have been transferred in from South East London garages including 10136 seen earlier on in Selkent Ambassador livery. The transferred vehicles however did receive a refurbishment before taking up the route. 19748 (NS) is certainly a newer vehicle than the passengers have been travelling on previously in the form of Arriva Volvo ALX400 VLAs, seen heading to Romford Station. Tuesday 15 October 2019.

Single deckers are usually the preserve of the 296 since 2001 when it was converted from double decker's but, more frequently these days it sees a few double deckers working the route throughout the day. The route was introduced in 1982 between Romford and Harold Wood Station, later extended in 1987 westwards to Ilford replacing routes 66A and 139. In October 2000, the route was truncated back from Harold Wood Station to Romford when new route 496 was introduced replacing that section. 36265 (NS) also a North Street bus is seen in Cranbrook Road. Tuesday 15 October 2019.

The successor of Eastern National took up route 462 when it was introduced in 1993 using Mercedes minibuses operated by Thamesway. This route serves roads that were a part of a proposal for an extended route 362 but the extension never went ahead, hence the introduction of this route instead. Barking's 36636 (BK) still adorns its branding long after abandonment, at the time probably a good idea but a big waste of money when you think of how the wasted money could have been invested more better into our bus network. Tuesday 15 October 2019.

For many years a resident of Sidcup, Abbey Wood, and the old and new Plumstead Garages, the 161 has seen a good and interesting variety of vehicles over the years. Between 1981 and 1984, the route was operated by a mixed fleet of crew vehicles in the form of crew MDs and RMs, with the MDs being replaced by crew operated Leyland Titans in 1982. The route's southern terminus is at Chislehurst in Kent which has some historic caves used as an air raid shelter during the Second World War. The caves have hosted music events before with Jimi Hendrix, The Who, and Rolling Stones having performed there. Sunday 17 November 2019.

Stagecoach East Kent have just recently introduced a new express coach service M2 between Canterbury-Hempstead Valley-Chatham-North Greenwich. These coaches offer Wi-Fi, power sockets, air-conditioning and charges what is probably a much cheaper ticket than the competing railways to the areas. 53705 takes a rest at North Greenwich before its fast run back to Canterbury. Sunday 17 November 2019.

The previous 257 in the North East London area replaced trolleybus route 557 between Chingford Mount and Liverpool Street, continuing beyond where the trolleybuses terminated to terminate at London Bridge. Today's 257 routing was introduced to replace the Chingford Mount to Stratford section of route 262 in November 1988. In 1992, the route was curtailed at Walthamstow Central Station, at the same time being awarded to Capital Citybus with their yellow liveried buses, after the collapse of London Buses' London Forest District. This route remained with Capital Citybus successor First for a good number of years before Stagecoach won the tender in 2005, allocated to Stratford Garage and later West Ham Garage. Stagecoach would go on to win back the tender from Go-Ahead in 2017 after a five-year absence, this time allocated to Leyton Garage. 10160 (T) is seen in Hoe Street, Walthamstow. Wednesday 11 December 2019.

Chapter 2

Arriva

The 59 for part of its life has acted as a supplementary route to the 159 and at certain times has reached as far out of London as the Chipstead Valley, and Godstone Garage. In 1999, route 59 operated between Streatham Hill, Telford Avenue and Euston Station sharing the road with the 159 as far as Lambeth North, where it diverges off via Baylis Road and Waterloo Road, serving Aldwych and Holborn. At this time, the route was the preserve of first generation DWs; VLA158 (BN) has escaped onto the 59 from the 159, for which it was delivered to replace the RM/RMLs. Thursday 1 August 2011. (*Terry Wong Min*)

The bendy buses on the 73 lasted for exactly seven years, replacing Routemasters that were withdrawn on Friday 4 September 2004, with the route also being reallocated from Tottenham Garage to a new one in Lea Valley close to Edmonton Ikea. The route is now a ridiculous shadow of its former self; once operating regularly between Stoke Newington and Hounslow Bus Station, in its glory days it even ventured as far south west as Kingston and Hampton Court, boasting an allocation of 107 buses in the peak in 1938. This route was converted back to double deck using the DW class but is now operated at present by LTs between Stoke Newington and Oxford Circus and allocated to Stamford Hill Garage. Bank Holiday Monday 29 August 2011.

The 397 was a new London route previously replacing routes 531 and 532 which were operated by Arriva Herts & Essex, who had a small base in Debden to store their buses. Their small 9.4m Plaxton Pointer Darts would lose their turquoise and cream livery for the red Arriva London livery of the time, when the route was transferred to Arriva London North into Edmonton Garage where it joined the 'W' routes. ADL61 (EC) was one of the original vehicles which lasted until they were withdrawn and replaced by new mini Plaxton Pointer Dennis Dart SLF's in 2012. This route is no longer with Arriva, from 2017 it was awarded to CT Plus using new Alexander Dennis E200 MMCs. ADL61 (EC) is seen on the Chingford Road. Thursday 8 March 2012. (*Terry Wong Min*)

The 724 began as a Northern Orbital Green Line route in 1966, originally between Romford and High Wycombe in 1966 using RFs. Today, it is still an orbital route 57 miles long between Harlow Bus Station and Heathrow Airport, with the average journey taking up to three hours one way. It serves what was the old London Country area in places such as Harlow, Hertford, Welwyn Garden City, Hatfield, St Albans, Watford, and Rickmansworth, some of those locations also having LT Garages. Allocated to Harlow and Ware Garages, this route is an Arriva Kent Thameside route but allocated to the two Essex garages who run it on their behalf. 3895 passes through Denham in Arriva Shires livery, however these buses originally carried a green livery when new. Wednesday 21 June 2017. (*Terry Wong Min*)

The 29 is still a busy route serving Green Lanes, Finsbury Park and Camden Road into Central London. This route once served as far north into Hertfordshire at South Mimms and has been allocated up to four garages all at once at points in time. In 1977, the route operated between Enfield and Victoria but by 1991 a curtailment would see it lose its Victoria terminus for Trafalgar Square, followed by a further chop in 1992 when the route was replaced north of Palmers Green by the introduction of the 329. HV128 (WN) loads up in Camden Road. Thursday 27 July 2017. (*Terry Wong Min*)

Route 38 was born on 16 June 1912 between Leyton Green and Victoria Station on Mondays to Saturdays only, allocated to Leyton Garage which opened on the same day the route was introduced. The 1930s to mid-60s saw the route's northern terminus go deep into Epping Forest, where it terminated at Epping Forest Wake Arms Pub. This was later cut back to the famous Chingford Royal Forest Hotel terminus in 1965 which was lost to the reshaping plan back in 1968. It was the last route in North London to have conductors losing them on 28 October 2005 to new bendy buses. The bendy buses gave way to double deckers again in 2009 before being joined by five new LTs that operated certain journeys trialled in crew mode. After proving a successful idea, this saw the introduction to this route and other routes of new LTs with conductors. LT179 (CT) gets punched up by one of its shed mates at Hyde Park Corner. Sunday 3 June 2018.

Route 19 was allocated to Battersea Garage for much of its life as a crew operated route and the last crew operated Routemasters ran for the last time on April Fool's Day, Friday 1 April 2005, when OPO buses took over. The route and buses later moved into Brixton Garage with a shared Norwood allocation until 31 March 2012, when the route was won on tender by Go-Ahead London General and moved into Stockwell. Arriva won the route back in 2017 where it was allocated to Tottenham Garage who used to have a share of the route previously. Here, HV270 (AR) serves Constitution Hill bus stop alongside Green Park on its way to Battersea, the route used to continue beyond Battersea to terminate at Tooting Bec. Sunday 3 June 2018.

The 243 replaced the 543/643 trolleybus route on 19 July 1961 following the same routing of those elegant, silent, and clean electric vehicles between Wood Green and Holborn, but today the route continues to Waterloo. The route terminates at the northern end next to where the old Eastern National bus garage stood where the well-know 1970s sitcom *On the Buses* filmed its garage scenes in Redvers Road, Wood Green. The route was solely allocated to Stamford Hill and gaining a part allocation at Wood Green in 1966 this would later be lost to Tottenham in 1971. Apart from a brief night allocation at Wood Green in 2010, this route has solely been operated out of Tottenham Garage since 1986. HV252 (AR) is on the Kingsland Road sporting this second incarnation of an all over ad for Michelin tyres. Not much work needed to be done for this ad, as it is mostly made up of the bus's actual colour. Sunday 16 September 2018.

The 370 previously was a London Country route allocated to Grays Garage operating between Tilbury Ferry and Romford Garage serving such Essex towns as Chadwell St Mary, Grays, Ockenden, and Corbetts Tey as well as Upminster and Hornchurch. This incarnation of the route between Lakeside Shopping Centre and Romford came about in November 2007 when the route came under TfL's route contracting. After the route started to get more and more popular it was converted fully to double deck in order to cope with the loadings using VLAs and later some withdrawn London DLAs. These were superseded by much newer DW's dispersed from Clapton Garage. DW204 (GY) is seen at Romford Station. Thursday 2 August 2018. (*Jimmy Sheng*)

The original W4 was introduced as a result of reshaping in 1968 between Winchmore Hill and Turnpike Lane but this was withdrawn in 1980. Today's W4 was introduced in 1991 between Wood Green and Tottenham Hale serving the Broadwater Farm Estate. In 1992, it was extended a short distance from Tottenham Hale to serve the Ferry Lane Estate replacing the 41. In 1997, it received a further extension beyond Wood Green to Oakthorpe Park. In 2011, there was a route swap between operators when First received the W4 and Arriva the W6, with Go-Ahead receiving the route upon the takeover of Northumberland Park. Arriva recently won the W4 back in February 2018 using new short MMC E200s, ENN53 (WN) is seen in Wood Green High Road and is allocated to Wood Green Garage now, previously being a Tottenham route. Monday 27 August 2018. (*Terry Wong Min*)

Upon the closure of Arriva Shires Garston Garage in 2018, the routes operated from there were scattered to some Arriva garages in the London area and route 340 was one of them. This route is now currently allocated to Palmers Green Garage. HV81 (AD) is going along Station Road, Edgware as it starts its journey to Harrow. Note the bus has a Wood Green (WN) code on its side; for many years Palmers Green has been an out station to Wood Green Garage with some routes and vehicles being shared and interchanged between the two. Sunday 7 October 2018.

Down the Cally. Route 259 replaced the 659 trolleybus on 26 April 1961 which in turn replaced the 59 tram in 1938 between Waltham Cross and Holborn Circus. All three routes operated out of the old Edmonton Garage in Tramway Avenue, which was a former Tram then Trolleybus Depot. Today this route is reallocated to a different Edmonton Garage which is more of a yard than a garage located off the North Circular Road. HV208 (EC) glides down Caledonian Road passing Caledonian Road & Barnsbury London Overground Station on its way to King's Cross where it has been curtailed at since 1998. These new hybrid buses are as close as you can get to experiencing a trolleybus when it pulls off in electric mode, before the diesel engine kicks in. Sunday 21 October 2018.

A long and winding route traversing through the south eastern corner of the London bus network, the **99** is a fast running route between Woolwich and Bexleyheath going the very long way around. After leaving Woolwich and Plumstead and climbing the very steep Bostall Hill, the route reaches the towns of Belvedere and Erith where Dartford's DW451 (DT) is seen heading in the direction of Erith Station. The route still has a bit of a way to go from here before it finally reaches Bexleyheath Town Centre. Friday 25 January 2019.

Arriva has been no stranger to purchasing Stagecoach vehicles as they have recently taken into stock some hybrid double deckers. They previously purchased some E200s to replace older buses on the 268 which they operated until the route was lost on tender to Metroline. Some of them have moved to Arriva's South London garages, like ENL107 (TC) which is now at South Croydon Garage seen working the 166 in country village scenery of Chipstead, still very much showing signs of its previous owner although it has since received Arriva seat moquette. Tuesday 26 February 2019. (*Terry Wong Min*)

A week after Stagecoach lost the route to Arriva, DW500 (EC) pulls off from the stop in Blackhorse Lane on its way to Stratford. The route never received new buses as such but received these batch of higher numbered DWs as well as some ex first VNs that Go-Ahead inherited when it took over Northumberland Park Garage. Arriva reclassified these buses as VLW901-909. The 158 was introduced in 1981 and serves a busy corridor between Stratford and Chingford Mount. Saturday 9 March 2019.

DW523 (AE) helps to promote Transport for London's Oystercard product as it passes Stoke Newington Common wearing this bright all over advert encouraging off peak travel. The 106 for many years did the long slog between Finsbury Park and Becontree Heath but was cut back to Poplar, terminating alongside Blackwall Tunnel in 1971. In 1972, it was converted to OPO DMS before reverting to crew operation in 1979. It would be converted back to OPO again permanently in 1982 and would see an extension to Asda on the Isle of Dogs. Whitechapel became its terminus where it still terminates to this day. Upon winning the tender from Stagecoach, this route has been based at Ash Grove Garage, which incidentally replaced the route's original garage at Hackney in the 1980s. Friday 22 March 2019.

In October 1998, Route 341 was introduced to replace the 171A between Northumberland Park Tesco and County Hall. In 2003, the route gained a night service numbered N341 but a year later in 2004 the 'N' suffix was dropped, and the route given a 24hr route status. On 15 June 2019, the 341 was diverted on a new routing away from New Fetter Lane, Chancery Lane, and Gray's Inn Road, and diverted via Fleet Street, Farringdon Street, Farringdon Road, regaining the route on Rosebery Avenue. HV258 (AR) has just turned into Farringdon Road on its way to Waterloo. Saturday 29 June 2019.

Route 41 has always been associated with the North East London area between Archway and at different times Ilford, until it was diverted away from there to Stratford when route 123 took over the section between Ilford and Tottenham Hale, under stage 6 of the trolleybus replacement programme the route was diverted to serve Stratford and the Victoria & Albert Docks instead before being cut back to Tottenham Hale in 1968. As well as the route alterations in the Tottenham area where the one way system on Broad Lane and Monument Way were made into two way roads, Archway has also seen the one way system gone and a new two way road layout created, resulting in the 41 terminating now at the first stop in Junction Road. DW541 (AR) has just kicked everyone off at the last stop. Tuesday 20 August 2019.

In September 2000, Arriva won Route 194 from Stagecoach Selkent, when it was allocated to South Croydon Garage. This garage previously operated this route during London Buses' subsidiary South London era and for six years had a flirtation with single deck operation using Leyland Nationals. The route reverted to double deckers in 1992, in the form of Leyland Titans, when the route was awarded to Selkent. In London Transport days, the parent route had three prefixed routes 194A/B/C, and the main route has differed slightly at different periods but today it serves between Lower Sydenham and West Croydon Bus Station. DW509 (TC) heads down the Addiscombe Road. Friday 21 September 2019.

With the current and yet to come route changes for the London area, the 48 has been withdrawn completely and the 55 extended back to Walthamstow Central Station in its place, as well as replacing the 48 between Shoreditch and Bakers Arms, both routes sharing the same roads. This route was introduced in the east in September 1968 and helped to replace two other routes, the 38A between Whipps Cross and Clapton, and the 35 between Leyton and Shoreditch. Allocated to Leyton Garage for much of its life, it gained a Walthamstow allocation between 1985 and 1988. Leyton would solely reign again until the route was lost to Arriva in 2017. DWs would work the route until converted to LT like Ash Grove's LT319 (AE) about to pull out of the stop in Shoreditch, advertising the TV series *The Politician*. Friday 21 September 2019.

Once a very good connection between Homerton Hospital and Tottenham Court Road, the 242 was cut back to St Paul's where it terminated on the one-way system by the Little Britain entrance to St Bartholomew's Hospital. The route has since been cut back further between St Paul's and Shoreditch and the route diverted to serve Aldgate Bus Station via Commercial Street, replacing the 67. Whether this was a good traffic objective is arguable as many of the passengers would have used the route directly to get to Oxford Street or the City area for work and leisure, but now must take two or even three buses. Friday 21 September 2019.

Enfield Island Village was built between 1997 and 2003 on a site previously occupied by the Royal Small Arms Factory and before 1994, the village was part of the Epping Forest District of Essex, but in the April of that year it was transferred to the London Borough of Enfield. Enfield's DW566 (E) has just come to the end of its long wandering journey across outer North London from Turnpike Lane. The 121's eastern terminus used to be Chingford, but this was replaced by a slightly altered 313 routing in 1982. Friday 4 October 2019.

HV64 (AD) was reregistered with the Routemaster registration mark WLT664 in 2016, which was originally carried by RM664 'The Silver Lady', which was delivered to London Transport in unpainted aluminium livery, in conjunction with trials that were also taking place at the time on London Underground cars. This bus was painted into this livery due to some Arriva staff winning awards and is seen not long into its journey to Palmers Green, North Circular Road, making a stop at Finsbury Square. The 141 replaced trolleybus route 641 on 8 November 1961 under stage 12 of the trolleybus replacement programme. Saturday 5 October 2019.

Arriva operate the 150 out of their Barking Garage in Ripple Road, not to be confused with Stagecoach's Barking Garage at Fair Cross. A brief period of single deck operation took place between 1993 and 1997 when Barking Garage operated it with smart looking Optare Deltas, a handful of which for a time wore a silver and red livery. Another colourful livery that was to adorn the route was the blue and green livery of Harris Bus but sadly the company went into administration in 1999. Arriva has for the best part of 2019 been refurbishing many of its buses that have come up for half-life refurbishment. These buses are identifiable not only by the fresh coat of gleaming red paint but also by the new style of Arriva logo seen here on T181 (DX) on its way to Becontree Heath. Monday 7 October 2019.

Trolleybus replacement route 123 replaced route 623 between Woodford and Manor House but projecting to Ilford on the 27 April 1960, partially replacing the 41 at the same time. Tottenham lost its share to Palmers Green in 1968 when the route was rerouted up to Enfield until 1977, when the route was cut back and the 29 extended to replace it. Route tendering saw the route awarded to Capital Citybus with their yellow buses. Arriva won the route in 2005 from First London and allocated to Tottenham Garage once again where it still resides today with a shared Edmonton allocation since 2014. DW580 (AR) represents the Tottenham share as it passes Valentines Park. Tuesday 15 October 2019.

Over recent decades, London's air quality has reached a very high level of pollution. In order to combat this, the Government Green Bus Fund was created so that Transport for London and operators could purchase new hybrid vehicles, to replace diesel vehicles mostly on routes that pass through Central London and the City areas. As newer hybrid and electric buses enter service, some of the older vehicles have been moved further out into the suburbs to replace conventional diesel buses there. HV4 (BN) is one such vehicle that started its life at Wood Green on the 141 before moving over to nearby Tottenham to join a new delivery of HVs on the 76 that had been built with some slight design differences from the original handful built. In 2019, this vehicle resides in Brixton and is caught on the 50 in Norbury Crescent, freshly overhauled. Friday 18 October 2019.

Thornton Heath has been home to the 255 since 1998 when it was introduced to replace part of the 60 between Streatham Garage and Clapham Common. The route was converted to low floor in 2003 with Plaxton Pointer Dennis Dart SLFs. They were later replaced by DAF Wrightbus Cadets in 2008, which gave way for the E200s like ENL52 (TH) seen here in Rowan Road, Mitcham. The 255 presently operates between Pollards Hill and Balham Station. Friday 18 October 2019.

This route is a very recent addition to the London bus network, introduced in July 2019 between Bexleyheath Shopping Centre and Woolwich High Street via Plumstead and Thamesmead. DW436 (DT) is a Dartford bus and has been refurbished. It used to be the case that new buses had to be ordered for when an operator took over the contract for a particular route but in recent times this rule has become more relaxed, which means slightly older buses still with some service life left in them can actually be refurbished and used for some new contracts. Saturday 19 October 2019.

In 1959, the 229 was extended from Bexleyheath to Woolwich in order to replace the 698 trolleybuses and had a joint Bexleyheath and Sidcup allocation until 1977. This route previously had an allocation of DMS in 1982 for a very short two months before replacement by newer Leyland Titans at Sidcup, who had sole allocation from 1977 until closure. Coincidentally, the T class returned to the route in 2016 but in the form of E400s like Dartford's T296 (DT) seen in Bexleyheath. When Go-Ahead operated the route it passed right outside its home shed at Bexleyheath. Saturday 19 October 2019.

New route 335 was introduced on the 26 October 2019 between Kidbrooke and North Greenwich serving the new Greenwich Ikea, using some HVs from one of its London area garages. The area just beyond North Greenwich Station now forms part of a large privately owned estate, where lots of housing and office buildings are being developed creating new roads in the process. One such new road is this one which has been named Pilot Busway where a handful of routes traverse after leaving the bus station. HV43 (DT) passes along the Pilot Busway under the watchful eye of a TfL building in the background. Sunday 17 November 2019.

The 192 has just recently returned to Arriva at the beginning of November 2019. Apart from Go-Ahead's operation of this route between 2014 and 2019 this route has predominantly been operated by Arriva including its predecessor company Leaside, which would be purchased by Arriva. Enfield's ENN59 (E) sits on the stand at Enfield where it has just arrived. Thursday 21 November 2019.

Between 1938 and 1942, the 144 provided a west to east service between Alexandra Park, which sits at the bottom of Alexandra Palace, and Ilford. In 1947, Turnpike Lane became its western terminus where it remained until 1977 when buses were extended, to make the hard slug up the steep Muswell Hill where it terminates in the middle of the Broadway on the specially constructed bus stand in the middle of the road. Chingford was favoured instead of Ilford for its eastern termini in 1988, when it replaced the 102A between Edmonton and Chingford which in turn replaced its parent route 102 on that section. Today's route 144 is the renumbered 144A which operated between Edmonton Green and Muswell Hill Broadway. HV61 (WN) makes an appearance on the route which is usually the preserve of DWs. Sunday 30 November 2019.

Arriva have just purchased 32 vehicles from Stagecoach in November 2019; some were originally used for route 53 but when that route was allocated further newer buses, they were used on other Plumstead Garage routes. They are now allocated to Palmers Green Garage for the 34 which has returned home after a period of being operated by Metroline out of Potters Bar Garage who used the same vehicle type on the route. These buses have retained their Stagecoach seat moquette and interior decor, the only changes being fleet numbers, operator logos, and garage codes applied. They have been classed into the HV class and this one is HV189 (AD) (former 13029) seen in Silver Street. Sunday 30 November 2019.

The 102 was introduced in 1934 connecting North East London/Essex with North West London. The famous Chingford Royal Forest Hotel was its eastern terminus for many years until reshaping in 1968 led to the abandonment of that terminus for nearby Chingford Station instead. 1991 saw a western extension from Golders Green Station to Brent Cross Shopping Centre. On Bank Holiday Monday 27 August 1979, this route saw Muswell Hill's Shillibeer liveried DMS2646 and Palmers Green RM2186 both appear on the route by coincidence for the benefit of enthusiasts to get their pictures, arranged by a well-known enthusiast and author who was the GGM at Palmers Green at the time. The 102 only gets as far east as Edmonton Green today which is where 'heritage' T5 (AD) is headed at Silver Street. Sunday 30 November 2019.

When London Transport implemented its Reshaping Plan in 1968, key hub areas saw drastic route changes and the renumbering of some routes. The W3 replaced route 233 between Finsbury Park Station and Northumberland Park Station on 7 September 1968. This route climbs the steep hills of Alexander Palace Way passing Alexandra Palace itself, giving a tremendous view of London at the top. Alexandra Palace was opened in 1873 but suffered a fire two weeks later; again, in 1980, another fire struck causing a great amount of damage. Thankfully it was restored again and is still in use today. There is an old myth that the land on which the palace stands was once the home of a gypsy travellers' site back in the 1800s who put a curse on the site when they were moved on for the palace to be built. Could that be what caused the two fires? Thursday 5 December 2019.

The 230 was a replacement for the section of route 241 between Stratford and Manor House in June 1973, it was allocated to Leyton Garage. Despite being allocated RMs this route saw a reprieve of the RT when it received a full allocation between 1976 and 1977 due to the spares shortages LT was experiencing during the 1970s. For a time, this route was converted to single deck operation but double deckers would return in 2004. Its long tenure at Leyton Garage would come to an end in 2013, when the route was awarded to Arriva and it was allocated to Tottenham Garage. DW542 (AR) is seen heading for Upper Walthamstow where it has terminated since 1996 after being diverted away from Leytonstone. Wednesday 11 December 2019.

Chapter 3

Go-Ahead

The Alexander Dennis ALX400 body came with many body designs and with two types of Chassis, the DB250LF and Volvo B7TL. Stagecoach was entirely equipped with DB250LF chassis', but Arriva and Go-Ahead took delivery of their versions with the Volvo B7TL chassis, London United receiving a mixture of both. Both Go-Ahead and London United were operators in common in ordering vehicles with this style of body with the centre staircase seen on AVL4 (Q) at Elephant and Castle. These were replaced by later batches of PVLs. Tuesday 6 November 2007. (*Terry Wong Min*)

The 425 was a new double deck route introduced on 5 July 2008 to partially replace the S2 between Stratford and Clapton, Nightingale Road and awarded to Go-Ahead London General. Until the new Scania Omnicity vehicles arrived for the route, veteran PVLs and Scania Omnidekkers were used, like weather beaten PVL184 (SI) seen on Lower Clapton Road. Buses tend to get grubby during the winter months and it would seem a pointless task to keep washing the buses nightly for it to get like this again the following day, even if it does mean the buses would look more presentable to the passengers. The route was extended in December 2018 to Ilford, and certainly helps the already busy 25 and 86. Sunday 11 January 2009.

The X68 is an express route between West Croydon and Russell Square making limited stops along some parts of the route operating northbound in the morning peak and southbound in the evening peak. This route was introduced in 1986 with Leyland Olympians from Norwood Garage. Go-Ahead have operated it since 2006 allocated to Camberwell Garage. It was allocated WVLs but PVLs like PVL308 (Q) has sneaked onto it occasionally seen in Whitehorse Lane, Selhurst. Wednesday 18 August 2010. (*Terry Wong Min*)

In 1959, route 170 replaced the 555 trolleybus in stage 2 of the conversion programme when it was extended beyond Hackney to terminate at Leyton Green. In October 1969, the route was cut back to Shoreditch and later to Bloomsbury, when new bus route 55 was introduced which coincidentally followed the same route as the 55 tram which the 555 replaced back in 1939. After a few changes to terminus and re-routings, the route now terminates at Victoria. LDP229 (SW) is standing at the last stop at the other end of the route in Roehampton, Danbury Avenue wearing a version of the Go-Ahead livery which has since disappeared and does look rather smarter than the complete all over red enforced today. Sunday 5 December 2010. (*Terry Wong Min*)

In 2009, the 376 was introduced, replacing parts of routes 276 between Prince Regent Lane and East Beckton and the 300 between East Beckton and Windsor Park Estate in the Cyprus area, operating between East Ham Town Hall and the new Beckton Bus Station that was built opposite Beckton DLR Station going the indirect way. Awarded to East London Bus Group, this route would later be taken on by Stagecoach when they bought back that operator along with its Selkent counterpart. Go-Ahead have operated it since 2011 using E200s which until 2018 were allocated to River Road Garage but were transferred in that year to nearby Silvertown Garage. SE98 (RR) is seen in Ron Leighton Way, built when East Ham High Street was pedestrianised and made one way with buses having the priority. Saturday 1 October 2011. (*Terry Wong Min*)

Go-Ahead Docklands Buses was awarded the D7 in 2011 when they took over from First London and allocated it to their garage at Silvertown, using new WVLs. When this route was introduced, it was operated by Leyland Titans provided by West Ham Garage on Mondays to Friday at first but in October 1992 upon the closure of West Ham the allocation moved into Bow. The following year, the route gained Sunday operation using Stratford Dennis Darts. Before going over to Go-Ahead, the route saw a twelve-year period with First Capital. WVL413 (SI) is seen at Limehouse. Sunday 19 February 2012. (*Jimmy Sheng*)

The 132 was extended from Eltham Station to North Greenwich in October 2009. This route has previously been operated by Boroline, Kentish Bus, Harris bus, TfL's in-house bus company East Thames Buses that took over from Harris Bus after the company went into administration before it became Go-Ahead. PVL154 (BX) is one of a batch used as a stop gap converting the route to double deck before the route received new E400s during the 2012 Olympics. Friday 7 November 2014.

In 1966, London Transport introduced their first Red Arrow route, numbered the 500, which during the peak ran express between Marble Arch and Victoria Station calling at very limited stops. This was the beginning of numerous Red Arrow services that provided short journeys between two points. To mark the 50th anniversary Go-Ahead's MEC50 was picked to be painted in a livery that the original MBA buses wore when introduced with the route, which included coin slot stickers to tell passengers to insert their coins in the box when boarding. There are stories told of buses on the 500 going around Hyde Park Corner and a box load of coins ending up sprawled over the road, because they came loose from the flimsy coin boxes and rolled out of the bus when it went over bumps in the road. This was also said to occur on Wood Green's 'W' routes who had the same vehicles. Saturday 9 April 2016. (*Jimmy Sheng*)

Route 1 was one of London's first motorbus routes introduced in November 1908 and was once a route that linked Lewisham with Willesden Garage in North West London. An extension from Catford Garage to Bromley took place in 1965 replacing the 199, but this was cut back to Catford Garage again in 1978. The route was converted to OPO Leyland Titans in 1987, these lasting until 1991 when they were ousted by Leyland Olympians. WHV vehicles like WHV157 (MG) on Waterloo Bridge replaced the VLWs in 2016 and is seen heading to Canada Water where it was extended in 1999 from Rotherhithe to a newly built Bus Station, which was incorporated into the new Jubilee Line Station. Tuesday 17 January 2017. (*Terry Wong Min*)

The only Red Arrow routes now left in London are the 507 and sister route 521. Both began service using MBAs which had very few seats as the short routes had a short journey time with a few stops. The 521 replaced parts of the 501 introduced in 1968, and the 513 that was introduced in January 1970 replacing the 13 between Aldwych and London Bridge. Both received Leyland National Mk2s in 1981 which went on to receive a major refurbishment making them last until 2002 when bendy buses took over. These were replaced by standard length Mercedes Benz Citaro but these have all been ousted with electric buses to make Waterloo Garage a 100 per cent electric garage. SEe8 (RA/Q) is one of these new vehicles with special branding on Waterloo Bridge telling people that its electric. Tuesday 17 January 2017. (*Terry Wong Min*)

As part of the Dagenham Dock and Barking Reach housing developments, a new bus network was created connecting those two areas with the Barking and Ilford areas and branded as the East London Transit (ELT). It started with two routes, the EL1 (Ilford Hill to Thames View Estate) replacing the 369, and EL2 (Dagenham Dock to Ilford Hill) both starting on 20 February 2010. A third route was later introduced on 18 February 2017 between Barking Reach and Little Heath, replacing the 387 numbered the EL3. All three routes are operated by Go-Ahead Docklands Buses, and the old order is seen here in the form of WVL334 (RR) a year before all three routes received LTs in the special branded livery worn by this WVL. The EL3 has since been diverted away from Little Heath to Becontree Heath. Thursday 16 February 2017.

Route 5 was one of the first routes to get a full allocation of the new RMs back in 1959 under stage 4 of the trolleybus replacement programme allocated to Poplar and West Ham Garages, in November 1959 operating between Bloomsbury Red Lion Square and Barking Garage. In 1971, the route was converted to OPO DMS lasting a decade before reverting to RMs again at West Ham Garage, with Barking providing Leyland Titans on Sundays shared with Upton Park DMS. In January 1981, the route's eastern terminus was East Ham White Horse and the route saw an extension beyond Bloomsbury down to Waterloo via the Aldwych. In April 1981, the route swapped East Ham White Horse for Becontree Heath where it remained until it took over the 87 route and was extended to Romford Market in 2006. WVL486 (RR) is seen in Rush Green Road. Thursday 19 April 2018. (*Terry Wong Min*)

The Monday to Saturday 15B was renumbered as the 115 on 18 September 1999 and only operated until a certain time in the evening, running alongside route 15 which was crew operated with Routemasters until the end of the evening peak, and a Sunday service also added. The buses from the 115 then worked the 15 when that route converted to OPO for the evening covering the entire length of the 15 and 115. In August 2003, the 115 was changed to operate all day instead of until the evening, replacing the 15's evening/night and Sunday extensions to East Ham, White Horse. Go-Ahead Blue Triangle obtained the route from Stagecoach in August 2017 where we see EH134 (RR) pulling into Canning Town Bus Station. Saturday 5 May 2018.

A route I remember well as it passed right in front of the flats where I lived and grew up for many years in East Ham, this new route was introduced in 1993 with East London Hoppa branding on the sides of the Metroriders between East Ham Station and Cyprus Windsor Park Estate. In 1999, it was diverted and extended at Prince Regent to connect with the new bus station built alongside the new Jubilee Line extension station at Canning Town. There was one incident remembered on the 300 that brought about buses having new engine air intakes having protective grills placed over the holes, due to young children in the Park Avenue and Folkestone Road areas of the route grabbing onto the back of the bus and riding on the back as the bus went along, which resulted in a serious incident involving a classmate's younger brother who fell off and hit his head on the road, resulting in him having to be air lifted to hospital whilst in a coma. SE40 (SI) is on the Barking Road. Saturday 5 May 2018.

In its heyday, the 101 could boast a whopping 64 RT during Monday to Friday with whispers that it could have reached 100. With the Royal Albert Docks still being very active up to the 1960s, the route was often operated in two overlapping sections due to buses getting held up and delayed when ships arrived in the dock to offload its cargo. The route for much of its life was associated with Upton Park Garage, which closed in 2011 with the route being reallocated to Barking. Stagecoach would lose the route in 2017 to Go-Ahead Blue Triangle whose WVL478 (RR) is wearing the striking East London Transit livery in which these vehicles operated on the EL1 and EL2 until LTs took over. This WVL has just recently migrated east from Stockwell Garage when seen as it still retains its SW garage code. Saturday 5 May 2018.

For some time, the 22 plied its trade between Putney Common and Homerton until 1987 when the route was withdrawn east of Bloomsbury during weekdays but still reaching Homerton on Sundays. A further cut-back to Piccadilly Circus took place in 1990. This route returned to Putney Garage in 1987 after replacing a short-lived Wandsworth allocation, which replaced its Battersea allocation when that garage closed a couple of years earlier. The route was taken away from Piccadilly Circus and diverted at Green Park to serve Berkeley Square and Conduit Street paralleling the C2 which has since been withdrawn to terminate at Oxford Circus. Sunday 3 June 2018.

Today the 155 parallels the Northern Line between Tooting and Elephant & Castle going in a straight south westerly direction. Between 1966 and 1971 on Sundays, the route went all the way to Hersham, where it replaced both the 131 and 264 that day. Wimbledon was its terminus until 1999 when it was diverted to serve Tooting, St George's Hospital. Some new vehicles entered service in 2015 replacing the PVLs that had served the route since 2003, WHV88 (AL) is seen at Stockwell heading southbound to Tooting. Monday 29 October 2018. (*Terry Wong Min*)

As well as taking part in trials between traditional crew operated RMLs and single door 'off the peg' Leyland Atlanteans and XF Fleetlines in 1966, this route also trialled the one and only front entrance, rear engine FRM Routemaster bus to be built which is preserved and owned by the London Transport Museum. This route was awarded to Go-Ahead in 2017 and was recently rerouted at Moorgate down London Wall, St Paul's Station, and New Change to St Paul's Cathedral. LT902 (NP) gets to the end of London Wall about to turn left into City Road. New buildings have sprung up replacing the older but not that much older buildings from the 1960s and 70s, like the one seen behind the bus. Saturday 29 June 2019.

The 200 has been a colourful route over the years adorning various operator liveries of Cityrama, Mitcham Belle, and Centra. It has seen a mixture of double and single deck allocations throughout its time from RTs and RFs to the SMS and DMS as well as stints with both Metrobuses and Leyland Nationals. In 1992, it was converted back to single deck whilst under London General ownership and given a Streetline branded livery. After losing it for a while to Mitcham Belle and Centra, the route returned to London General in 2006 who still operate it today. SE4 (AL) loads up in Mitcham High Street. Wednesday 13 March 2019. (*Terry Wong Min*)

LT50 (SW) was given a reincarnation of this version of General livery seen passing on the Wandsworth Road. This road is likely to get busier once the Nine Elms extension on the Northern Line opens with the many apartments being built alongside on a vast site. This livery is even more striking as it glistens in the sunshine. Thursday 11 April 2019. (*Jimmy Sheng*)

During the Wimbledon tennis fortnight, many spectators flock to Wimbledon and the surrounding area at Southfields to get to the tournament. The 93 helps move the large numbers as well as the special tennis shuttle routes that operate from Wimbledon, Southfields, and Central London. DOE32 (A) descends Wimbledon Hill to North Cheam. This route used to terminate at Epsom Clock Tower but this section was replaced by new route 293 in April 1970. Friday 12 July 2019.

Newly introduced in 2003 using LDP Plaxton Pointers, this route had some route branding at Cantrail level on its buses. This route has trialled several experimental Electric and hybrid buses in recent years and is now operated by these electric SEe buses, the small 'e' denoting that it is an electric version of the ADL E200 MMC product. SEe62 (Q) rounds St George's Circus coming to the end of the route. Tuesday 23 July 2019.

During both world wars, women came to the aid of the country and filled jobs that were said to only be able to be done by men whilst the men were away fighting for king and country. On 1 November 1915, Mrs G. Duncan became the first female clippie in London when she joined the Thomas Tilling Company working on the 37. After the Second World War, women would be allowed to apply for roles with London Transport as conductresses, but it wasn't until 1974 that it got its first woman bus driver when Jill Viner passed out at Chiswick aged 22; the Underground would be a few years later in 1978 when Hannah Dadds passed out as motorman on the District Line. Peckham E257 (PM) pulls out of Acre Lane, Brixton. Thursday 25 July 2019.

Recently won from Metroline, the 214 now operates with new SEes based at Northumberland Park Garage, where electric charging points have been installed to recharge the vehicles. The St Pancras area of this route has changed out of all recognition since the regeneration of the area ready for it becoming the terminus of Eurostar and the South Eastern High Speed line. SEe86 (NP) passes beneath the Midland Main Line on Pancras Road. Tuesday 20 August 2019.

With the withdrawal of route C2, the 88 has seen an extension along the former route from Camden Town to Parliament Hill Fields, but due to the turning point being too tight up at Parliament Hill Fields, the 87 has had its buses swapped with the LTs from the 88. EH305 (SW) passes Camden Gardens as it travels south to Clapham Common. This route originally followed a West to South alignment between Acton Green and Mitcham and remained crew operated until 1992. Between 1993 and 1997, the route was operated with single deckers and branded as the 'Clapham Omnibus' but high patronage would see double decker's return. The western end of the route between Oxford Circus and Acton Green was replaced with new crew route 94. Sunday 25 August 2019.

Route 378 is a new route introduced to South West London on 3 August 2019. Upon the closure of Hammersmith Bridge in April 2019 preventing any road vehicles except bicycles to be able to pass over it, route 209 had a rerouting with the route diverted at Barnes Pond to terminate at Putney Bridge. The 209 was later rerouted back to its original routing towards Hammersmith Bridge and the 378 introduced instead between Mortlake and Putney Bridge. Unusually, the 378 and 209 share a joint schedule meaning that the drivers and buses are actually used on both routes, with a 378 leaving Putney Bridge and getting to Mortlake, then working a 209 from Mortlake to Castelnau which is the terminus south of Hammersmith bridge, then working back to Mortlake as a 209, then turning into a 378 for its return journey back to Putney Bridge. SE293 (AF) travels down Lower Richmond Road. Sunday 25 August 2019.

In 1934, route 21 went from Turnpike Lane all the way to Farningham in Kent close to Sevenoaks. It has been allocated to six garages before now at New Cross where it is still allocated, Sidcup, Old Kent Road, Camberwell, West Green, and Catford, only Camberwell, Catford, and New Cross still being operational garages today. In January 2006, the route took its current form when it was extended from Finsbury Square sharing the road with route 141 as far as Newington Green where it terminates. December 2016 would see the route start to be converted to LT. LT850 (NX) is on the City Road. Bank Holiday Monday 26 August 2019.

The Orpington area R routes were introduced in the late 1980s as minibus routes operated by a new company called Roundabout, and today there are up to 11 R routes that either serve or connect with other R routes that centre on Orpington. This was later taken over by First who branded it as Orpington Buses. Metrobus won the tender in 2007 and today it is operated under Go-Ahead who bought the small but successful Metrobus outfit. WS3 (MB) is seen on the R3 in Towncroft Lane and is a Wright bodied Street lite. Such small vehicles cope well with small outer suburb routes such as this that serve some back streets as hail and ride service. Friday 21 September 2019.

Also in Towncroft Lane at Petts Wood is EH318 (MB). Route 208 has recently been won from Stagecoach in July 2019 after a 33 year stint in the Selkent district, with both Catford and Bromley sharing the allocations. Towards the end, Bromley had the sole share of the route. Passengers to this route had recently got new E400s two years before, replacing Stagecoach's Dennis Tridents and were treated to further new buses when Go-Ahead took over. Lewisham is the route's northern terminus. Friday 21 September 2019.

The 119, also a former Metrobus route, brought a touch of brightness to the Croydon area with its blue and yellow liveried buses when it was won from Stagecoach in 1998 bringing about an end to its long association with Bromley Garage. WHV53 (C) heads for Bromley North. The bus's blind box is not very readable when the sun is at certain points in the sky due to the shadow being cast onto the blind, which is positioned further back into the blind box than previous bus builds. Friday 21 September 2019.

In 1934, the 35 terminated at Highams Park Station in the Essex countryside but was later extended to Chingford Hatch. In September 1968, instead of going via Kingsland Road, Dalston Junction and Dalston Lane, it was rerouted between Shoreditch and Hackney via Cambridge Heath, replacing the 257 in the process, emerging opposite Clapton Pond where it continued on to Chingford. From 1982, it ran between Clapton Pond (Hackney Station on Sundays) and Clapham Common and the route was still crew operated with traditional buses throughout before it fell to OPO in 1986 with Leyland Titans, and extended from Clapham Common to Clapham Junction. A brief rerouting took place from Clapton Pond to Homerton Hospital in 1987, but today we see EH118 (Q) standing at the Shoreditch terminus where it has terminated since November 1991. Friday 21 September 2019.

The 396 connects Ilford with King George's Hospital in Goodmayes travelling along the Eastern Avenue between Gants Hill and Little Heath. The original King George's Hospital was sited close to Newbury Park and was opened in July 1931 by George V, but this was closed in 1993 when a new hospital was opened on a new site on Barley Lane. Go-Ahead Blue Triangle won this route from Stagecoach in March 2019 and just like the previous operator, the occasional double deck vehicles stray onto the route in the form of some ex Merton E400s. SE117 (RR) is the regular order of the day travelling into Ilford. Tuesday 15 October 2019.

Stockwell Garage's E138 (SW) is unique to the fleet in that it received a new roof after its previous one was deroofed under a low bridge; it is working the 118 to Morden on Rowan Road. One of the oddities of the 1990s saw this route demoted to midibus operation in the evenings on a Monday to Saturday. This route has been allocated to Stockwell Garage since 2017. Friday 18 October 2019.

The 80 lost its double deck SOE vehicles in 2015 for single deck E200s when the contract was renewed. This route has been allocated to Sutton Garage since 1934, and its current routing dates to 1996 when the route was extended from Morden to Hackbridge to replace withdrawn route 393. This resulted in the Belmont to Banstead section being withdrawn and replaced by the S1. SE270 (A) passes along Middleton Road. Friday 18 October 2019.

In 1951, route 180 replaced tram route 36 operating between Catford Garage where the route was allocated and Woolwich, with a Monday to Friday peak hour and Saturday afternoon extension to Plumstead Common. In 1963, the route gained an allocation from Abbey Wood Garage to complement the Catford share which lasted until the new Plumstead Garage opened in 1981, taking the whole allocation from both. This route has seen a few trial buses in its time including a Leyland articulated vehicle based at Catford, as well as an Optare Delta Demonstrator, and a tri-axle vehicle loaned from Capital Citybus. The route came to Go-Ahead in 2009 and the current vehicles are these second generation WVL's, WVL325 (MG) crosses over the railway lines which some form part of the new Crossrail line. Saturday 19 October 2019.

Also at Abbey Wood, the 244 serves a stop by the entrance to the station at a lower level down beside the main station entrance as well as on the bridge above. SE83 (BX) is turning into Abbey Wood Road underneath the bridge which it is about to pass over. Saturday 19 October 2019.

The 286 has gained some new vehicles recently in the form of WS's, originally delivered for the 170 at Stockwell. However, due to a bridge height and turning restrictions, standard E200s were allocated to the route instead. Wright Street Deck WS109 (MG) is seen in Eltham heading for Queen Mary's Hospital in Sidcup. Saturday 19 October 2019.

Route 89 operates between Lewisham and Slade Green Station where it connects with the 99. The route for a time had a shared New Cross and Bexleyheath allocation but today its solely allocated to Bexleyheath and passes outside its home garage along the route. E51 (BX) has just begun its journey to Lewisham and will ascend the bridge over the South Eastern line that serves the station. Saturday 19 October 2019.

In 2003, the southern section of route 36 between New Cross and Lewisham was withdrawn and replaced by new bendy bus route 436, with both serving the same route between New Cross and Paddington, where the 436 terminated. It wasn't uncommon to see 36s running almost empty whilst everyone waited to board 'the free bus'. With the building works at Victoria Station taking place, through buses were unable to serve their stop in Victoria Bus Station, due to work site portacabins being set over the road area. Buses were subsequently diverted around via Bressenden Place then back to line of route in Vauxhall Bridge Road. EH231 (NX) is seen in Bressenden Place about to pass one of the new entrances built for Victoria Underground Station. Wednesday 13 November 2019.

Stockwell's LT60 (SW) received this incarnation of the 1933 General livery for the Year Of The Bus in 2014 and is still seen wearing it making it stand out from the rest, along with stablemate LT50 which also has a distinct livery. The 11 has always been known as a tourist route because it passes many sights like St Paul's Cathedral, Fleet Street, Royal Courts of Justice, Trafalgar Square, Big Ben and the Houses of Parliament at Westminster. Here at Trafalgar Square, one of the lions watches it on its way to Liverpool Street. Friday 15 November 2019.

MEC1 (NX) is the first vehicle of a batch of buses delivered in 2009 to replace the bendy buses on Red Arrow routes 507 and 521 with the vehicle starting on the 507 first with that route being converted in July 2009. After both the 507 and 521 received new electric buses, the MECs were allocated to the 108 replacing the DWLs that were inherited from when Go-Ahead took over East Thames Buses. Route 108 has served between Lewisham and north of the river to East London for many years and was once a double deck route until the rebuilding of the Blackwall Tunnel meant the northbound tunnel was rebuilt to a lower height that meant double deckers would not be able to use it. The southbound tunnel can still fit a double deck through it and has been used by Jubilee Line rail replacement buses before. Sunday 17 November 2019.

The 129 route number for many years was used for an East London route between Claybury and Becontree Heath, but when this route was replaced by an extended route 128, the number has since been reused in South East London as a local route between North Greenwich Station and Greenwich. It started out as single deck but was converted to double deck in 2016 and there is talk of the route being extended to Peckham, but whether this comes to fruition is another matter. WVL354 is dwarfed by the big developments that have sprung up in North Greenwich what look very American in design. Sunday 17 November 2019.

The 191 is a meandering route between Edmonton Green and Brimsdown today, interchanging with three London Overground stations on the way at Edmonton Green, Southbury, and Enfield Town additionally serving Enfield Chase and Brimsdown National Rail stations. In days gone by, this route used to serve the Chingford area but this ceased in 1982. EN5 (NP) picks up in Chase Side close to Enfield Chase Station and is an ex-First London vehicle at Northumberland Park denoted by the 'N' in its fleet number. Friday 22 November 2019.

Chapter 4

Metroline

Although this book is focused predominantly on day routes of which many are now 24hrs, at least one night bus route deserved an inclusion. On Sundays, this route finished late in the morning meaning in summer it was possible to see buses operating in the daylight. This shot was taken at 08:14, when the day buses have been in service for a couple of hours and all the night buses have finished for the night, as TE927 (HT) passes Finchley Central Station for Barnet Church. The driver will have to travel empty back south to Holloway Garage where it has passed on its journey at Archway. Sunday 1 July 2012. (*Terry Wong Min*)

Passport to Pimlico. Route 38 was the first route in London to trial out the New Bus For London in service in crew mode, using 5 LTs with drivers as conductors, but the honour fell to route 24 to become the first fully converted LT route daily when the route was won back from Go-Ahead London, with conductors being on board from 05:05 for most of the day, with the last crew bus finishing just after 21:00 with the rest of the night being OPO. Conductors were later given the weekends off and only worked to a Monday to Friday schedule. LT99 (HT) has just passed the Cenotaph in Whitehall on its way to Pimlico with one of the conductors illustrating the rear open platform, designed like the Routemaster and its predecessors to aid boarding and alighting in traffic to help prevent long dwell times at bus stops. Wednesday 10 September 2014. (*Terry Wong Min*)

Metroline operated two varieties of the Plaxton President in its fleet. The VP/VPL had Volvo B7TL engines whilst the TP/TPL versions had DAF DB250 engines making them sound like Dennis Tridents. VPL584 (HT) was the last of several hanging on at Holloway Garage at this time but its time is nearly up at this point, leaving Willesden and Harrow Weald Garages as the last posts with their small handful of VPs left, though these were gone by mid-December 2019. The 4 no longer serves Waterloo but instead terminates at Blackfriars Station via Queen Victoria Street. St Paul's Cathedral serves as a nice backdrop for the picture and is an icon for surviving the heavy London Blitz of 1940/41 whilst much of the buildings around it were destroyed and remained bomb sites up until the 1960s/70s. Sunday 26 March 2017.

The busy 16 used to continue beyond Cricklewood Garage where it finishes today to terminate at Sudbury Town Station until June 1970. In October 1997, new route 316 took over the section beyond Cricklewood Garage to Neasden Tesco, but this in turn was later taken over by the 332 which runs alongside the 16 between Edgware Road Station and Cricklewood Garage, taking some of the load off the 16. LT190 (W) was delivered new to Holloway Garage in 2014 for the 24 and 390 when it was the fastest LT there and hardly had any mechanical faults with it like the others did. It later moved over to Cricklewood Garage for a time but has since returned to Holloway Garage. Sunday 9 April 2017. (*Jimmy Sheng*)

The 52 recently received new VWHs to replace its VWs that ousted older VPLs. The 52 today operates to a routing between Willesden Garage and Victoria Station, but before 1992, the route continued northwards to Mill Hill Broadway. From 1981, the 52 had a newly introduced suffix route numbered the 52A between Victoria Station and Westbourne Park Station, after a few alterations to termini this route was withdrawn in 1991. VWH2309 (AC) travels through the North West London suburbs approaching Kensal Rise Station. Sunday 25 February 2018. (*Terry Wong Min*)

In order to try and combat traffic congestion and try and improve reliability of the bus network, the central area of London has seen and has yet to see some changes to the network. One change we have seen in recent years is the rerouting of the 6 away from Oxford Street and Regent Street via Park Lane, Piccadilly, and Piccadilly Circus where it picks up its routing to the Aldwych at Piccadilly Circus. Here we see Willesden's VWH2312 (AC) serving Green Park, Constitution Hill stop which has now been moved further up the road closer to Hyde Park Corner, heading for its home garage. Sunday 3 June 2018.

Route 32 in 2018 was allocated E400s out of Cricklewood Garage until this route was reallocated to Edgware Garage a week or so after this picture was taken. However, whilst the route was allocated at Cricklewood, it became quite common for an LT or two to be put out on the route. Here at the stop before its then home garage, we see LT557 (W) heading south to Kilburn Park in a Banana advert livery which certainly stands out from the usual red. The LT class have practically become advertising buses, seeing more adverts applied than to any other vehicles in use. Saturday 21 July 2018.

The C11 was London Transport's first midibus route back in 1972 operated Monday to Saturday between Archway Station and Cricklewood Broadway using Ford Strachan midibus vehicles (FS Class), very small size vehicles by London Transports standards at this period. The route was extended to Willesden Green in 1976 but in 1982 would take a new routing to terminate at West Hampstead, West End Green with a southern projection beyond Archway down to King's Cross following today's 390 routing. DE869 (W) departs Brent Cross where it has served since 1984 at the start of its journey south to Archway which is as far south the routes gets today. Thursday 8 August 2018. (*Terry Wong Min*)

Starting as an outer suburbs route between Hendon Central Station and Mill Hill Broadway in 1934, it was later extended to Canons Park where it ran alongside trolleybuses on route 645. On 18 October 1939 during the 'Phoney War' in the Second World War, the route become a trunk route operating between Edgware Station and Oxford Circus via the Finchley Road. At Edgware Station, we see TEH1237 (EW) swinging into the road leading to the more recent bus station. It is hard to imagine that buses used to park up on the station forecourt just to the left of the bus. The 113 in September 2019 continues to be a connection between Edgware and London's Oxford Street and has recently saw Baker Street and Gloucester Place become two directional. Sunday 7 October 2018.

Climbing its way up towards Totteridge VMH2045 (PB) is almost close to the end of its journey from Winchmore Hill to Finchley Central around the outer North London Suburbs which includes a stop at the 1930s-built Art Deco Underground station, built by Charles Holden at Southgate on the Piccadilly Line that got renamed 'Gareth Southgate' briefly during the 2018 World Cup. These form the contingent of other hybrid vehicles in the London fleet to make London's air less polluted. Sunday 17 October 2018.

Today's incarnation of route 46 began in 1972 between Hampstead Heath and Farringdon Street, replacing the northern portion of route 45. From 1982 onwards, the route's terminus was pushed further west starting with Kensal Rise Station, then Warwick Avenue station, until in 2007 it was extended to Lancaster Gate Station. With rebuilding works in the City area, the eastern terminus has also been changed from Farringdon Street, Stonecutter Street to St Bartholomew's Hospital in 2013, where we see BEL2508 (HT) heading. The BELs are new electric single deckers and due to the route's original garage at King's Cross being insufficient to install charging points, the route was reallocated to Holloway Garage where the charging points were able to be installed. Sunday 21 October 2018.

LT16 (HT) was one in the original batch of LTs delivered to Holloway Garage for the re-introduction of crew operation on route 24 in 2013. With the subsequent conversion of route 24 and 390 back to OPO in 2016 and the conversion of route 91 from TEs to LTs the vehicles have become interworked on occasions as seen here in Caledonian Road where it has wandered off route onto the 91. The 91 is allocated a batch of LT in the 7xx series and the only short example of LT in the form of ST812, the main differences between later and early batches being the rear door slides open outwards along the body side as opposed to the conventional inwards which was designed to be locked open during crew mode. Sunday 21 October 2018.

The 274 began as a double deck route in 1991 using Leyland Titans out of Chalk Farm Garage but was converted the following year to single deck Dennis Darts and the route remained single deck throughout until late 2018. The route was given double deckers when the route's contract was extended for a further two years with Metroline. The VMHs like VMH2478 (KC) passing Caledonian Road & Barnsbury Station couldn't actually start operating the full route due to the need to cut back trees along the route, but the occasional one or two operated short journeys between Marble Arch and London Zoo which partially mimicked the zoo route 74Z of years past. Sunday 21 October 2019.

The 316 has been cut back and extended over its existence. Originally introduced in 1997 between Neasden Brent Park Tesco and North Kensington St Charles' Hospital, the route beyond Cricklewood garage would be replaced by the introduction of new route 332 (Paddington to Neasden Tesco) in 2008. It would gain an extension however a year later when it was extended from North Kensington to the newly built White City Bus Station, next to the new Westfields Shopping Centre which is where DEL2069 (W) is heading. DEL2069 (W) swings round at Ladbroke Grove Sainsbury's. Sunday 21 October 2018.

In 2016, new route 483 partly replaced the section of route 83 between Alperton Station and Ealing Hospital and routed via Wembley Central and Northwick Park Hospital to terminate at Harrow Bus Station. VW1270 (ON) is allocated to Alperton and has just set out from Harrow in the autumn evening sunshine on a trip to Ealing Hospital. Sunday 17 November 2018.

The 263 began life in 1971 replacing the northern end of trolleybus replacement route 104 between Barnet Church and North Finchley, it paralleled the 104 as far as Archway on weekdays, and Holloway, Nags Head at Weekends. The 104 was withdrawn in 1985, but today's 263 follows its exact routing from Barnet Church to Highbury Corner. Metroline won route 263 from First in 2002 and was allocated to Potters Bar Garage from where it still operates today. This route, like the 307, also serves Barnet Hospital and got an extension at its southern end in 2014 from Holloway, Nags Head to Highbury Barn. It subsequently got cut back to Highbury Corner but the short extension back around the corner to Highbury Barn was reinstated in 2017. TE1439 (PB) loads up at its first stop in North Finchley. Sunday 25 November 2018.

Uxbridge has many routes that serve and start from the bus station that radiate off in all directions including out of London into places such as Berkshire, as well as the long 724 route that runs between Harlow and Heathrow Airport. The A10 is one of them and is based at the nearby garage next door to Uxbridge Station which was inherited when Metroline gained several of First London's garages, routes, and vehicles in the big sell off. DE1803 (UX) makes a stop at Greenway. Saturday 22 December 2018.

Usually the preserve of the VW class, as does happen vehicles get used on other routes than the one for which they are intended. Metroline had already run this route for a stint between 1993 and 1998 before it was lost to Sovereign. Before Metroline gained the route in 1993, some very colourful buses and unusual vehicles were used by London Country North West whose Leyland Olympians and Atlanteans worked the route in their green with white band livery. A strike by that company in the late 1980s would also see coaches used supplied by Borehamwood Coach Services for a month. TE985 (EW) crosses the High Street to serve Elstree & Borehamwood Station. Saturday 24 August 2019.

On 3 October 1934, the newly created London Passenger Transport Board (London Transport) renumbered the 607 to 107. When the route was converted from crew operation to OPO in 1970, it received an allocation of Single Deck MBs which originally operated on the Red Arrow routes in Central London, before receiving an allocation of the unreliable DMS class two years later. These would last until 1981 when the more reliable Metrobuses arrived which gave good service until 1989. Metroline would gain the route in 1994 using single deck Plaxton Pointer Dennis Darts at Edgware Garage. Edgware's TE987 (EW) swings into the bus station alongside Elstree & Borehamwood Station. Saturday 24 August 2019.

The 84 was a unique route in that in LT days, it served London Transport's Country and Central areas of the bus network, making it possible to be operated by either department. Between 1982 and 1986, it was operated by London Country North East from St Albans Garage. From 1956 until its OMO conversion in 1969, the route was projected beyond Arnos Grove to terminate at Walthamstow on Sundays. Predominately a double deck route for much of its life, 1969-75 and 1979-80 saw it worked with MB/SMSs. In recent times, E200s have served the route in their special commercial livery but lately the route has started to see E400s used as well; with the loadings on this route, it should be converted back to double deck fully. This route as well as the 242 (Potters Bar Station to Waltham Cross) are operated by Metroline as commercial routes out of Potters Bar Garage, and are not as such run on behalf of London Buses, the 84 does pierce into the London area at Barnet. Saturday 24 August 2019.

The 31 along with sister route 28 saw some controversy in 1989 when the two routes were converted from Routemasters to single deck Wright bodied Dennis Darts running to high frequencies, but despite this, many passengers were still said to get left behind at the stop waiting for the next bus. After 15 years, someone in charge must have seen sense to convert the route back to double deck; the number of passengers waiting for the bus at the Camden Town Station stop is enough proof to show the need for double deckers. 2018 saw the route won by Metroline and operated out of their Perivale West Garage whose VW1190 (PA) is seen in Camden Gardens. The other end of the route terminates at White City Bus Station. Sunday 25 August 2019.

The 134 has recently gained some of these electric buses in the form of OMEs at Potters Bar and at least two of them are experimenting with electric dot matrix blinds. This is said to be London's first fully electric route along with the 43 bringing about zero emissions. In Camden Gardens, OME2655 (PB) heads for Warren Street, the cut back terminus of the route; this route used to continue down Gower Street to terminate at the bottom end of Bloomsbury Street close to the Shaftesbury Theatre, although Tottenham Court Road Station was stated on the destination blind. Sunday 25 August 2019.

The large Holloway Garage gained more electric buses to their allocation back in the summer; BDE2623 (HT) glides along silently on the City Road. Before Holloway gained the 43, the route was operated by Finchley and Muswell Hill Garages which both closed in the 1990s. In 1940, this route used to venture further south of the river on Sundays to Croydon Airport before getting cut back to London Bridge in 1941, where it still terminates. Bank Holiday Monday 26 August 2019.

Marble Arch sees Willesden Garage's BYD 1474 (AC) on the 98 where it terminates on the garage forecourt in Pound Lane. The route has an allocation of VWH vehicles that also interworks with the batches on the 6 and 52 but this route has a handful of these electric vehicles, which have batteries that apparently can power the bus for 20 hours before they need charging. The vehicle carries some green leaf vinyls which were also applied to some other earlier hybrid vehicles in the London fleets of other operators when they first entered service. These vehicles have since been withdrawn. Bank Holiday Monday 26 August 2019.

The 30 is a new acquisition for Metroline, winning the route from Tower Transit in June 2018 and is its only route that ventures into East London at Hackney Wick. The route is allocated to King's Cross Garage, which saw a shuffle round of routes with the 46 being moved back to Holloway where electric charging points have been fitted to charge its electric buses, and the loss of the 214 making room for the 30. VMH2488 (KC) goes around Marble Arch to its stand. Bank Holiday Monday 26 August 2019.

Just like the 32 previously, the 332 now sees a handful of Cricklewood's LTs appear throughout the whole week. The 332 was a new route introduced in 2007 between Paddington Station and Neasden Brent Park Tesco replacing a section of route 316, between Cricklewood Garage and Neasden using E400s but these were replaced with hybrid versions of E400 in 2014. This route travels for much of its journey up the busy Edgware Road, interchanging with the Bakerloo Line at Paddington, Edgware Road, and Maida Vale, London Overground at Kilburn High Road and Brondesbury, and the Jubilee Line at Kilburn. LT545 (W) has arrived at Brent Park Tesco. Bank Holiday Monday 26 August 2019.

The 237 for many years was an RF route both in crew then OPO mode, between 1953 and 1977 when these trusty buses were replaced by new Bristol BL. The 237 was later cut back from Chertsey Station to Sunbury Village, but extended from Hounslow whose RMs were transferred to Stamford Brook to reintroduce crew operation to this route, up to Shepherd's Bush replacing the 117. The 117 continued to parallel it as far as Brentford. VW1070 (AH) is at the Turnham Green end of Chiswick High Street. Sunday 8 September 2019.

The 266 replaced trolleybus route 666 under the penultimate stage 13 in the trolleybus replacement programme on 3 January 1962 between Edgware and Hammersmith. Many stories have been told by older London Transport staff who knew drivers and conductors who were very superstitious who refused to drive the 666 route, and even vehicles with the fleet number 666. The 266 now operates between Brent Cross Shopping Centre and Acton Old Town hall, and after just a few years of winning this route back from Tower Transit, Metroline will soon be giving over the route to RATP London United not long after this picture was taken. Sunday 8 September 2019.

Express route 607 carries the same route number of ex-Uxbridge Road trolleybus route 607 but didn't directly replace it, although the routing between Shepherds Bush Green and Uxbridge is the same original route as the trolleys. This busy route is a useful one, serving Acton, Ealing, Hanwell, Southall and Hayes along the way but leaving many of the local stops to the local buses. The route is an express version of the original 207 route introduced in 1960. Here at Bromyard Avenue in Acton Vale Greenford's VMH2591 (G) has escaped onto the route. Bromyard Avenue is also a turning point for late running buses on a few routes operating along this road when needed. Sunday 8 September 2019.

Introduced in 2008 to serve the new Heathrow Terminal 5 the 482 replaced much of route 435, and the H23, operated by Transdev (later London United RATP Group) using Scania Omnicities. Metroline took the route over in 2015 where it is allocated to Greenford Garage, an ex-First garage. TE1718 (G) is the order of the day on the Bath Road. Sunday 8 September 2019.

Metroline has recently opened a new garage on a new site in Brentford where the E8 is allocated. This route began as a minibus route but since 2016 has been operated by VW double deckers. This route has also since been extended beyond Brentford to Hounslow, Bell Corner. VW1260 (AH) is an ex-Holloway motor and is seen on the London Road in Isleworth and will soon be entering Hounslow past the garage and one-time bus station. Sunday 8 September 2019.

The current form of route 235 was introduced in 1996 to replace the western section of route 237 and was allocated to Hounslow Garage who used Metrobuses for the route. This route was operated for a time by Armchair who coincidentally was bought out by Metroline, but it wasn't until 2017 that Metroline gained this route from Abellio. DEL2253 (AH) is also seen in Isleworth. Sunday 8 September 2019.

The W8 was introduced by London Transport in 1969 as a new flat fare route replacing route 128 between Chase Farm Hospital and Lower Edmonton Station, using MBSs, and was later extended from Edmonton Green to Picketts Lock Centre (today's Lea Valley Leisure Complex) in 1973. Under First Capital guardianship, Metrobuses painted into the revised red and yellow livery were used, but these were replaced the following year by low floor Plaxton President bodied Tridents. Metroline gained this route in 2003 allocated to Potters Bar where their predecessor London Northern also allocated the route when they operated it. TE1425 (PB) picks up in Baker Street, Enfield. Thursday 21 November 2019.

From Saturday 7 December 2019, route 140 was withdrawn between Hayes & Harlington Station and Heathrow Airport Central Bus Station; this section was replaced by new route 278. Additionally, new express route X140 operates between Harrow Bus Station and Heathrow Airport Central Bus Station serving limited stops in between. Night bus route N140 has been introduced following the old 140 routing between Harrow Weald Garage and Heathrow Airport Central Bus Station. VWH2237 (HD) serves Harrow & Wealdstone Station where it provides a good interchange with the Bakerloo Line, London Overground Watford DC Lines, and London Midland. Sunday 8 August 2019.

The U3 was introduced as a new midibus route in 1989 using Mercedes Benz minibuses between Uxbridge and West Drayton Station where it did a loop down some roads. In 1993, it was made more into a point to point route and extended to Heathrow Airport via the withdrawn route 223. This route has remained single deck throughout until now, but one double deck was allocated from 2010. In 2017, the double deck vehicle allocated was a VP but now these are all now withdrawn an E400 is allocated instead. TE1736 has just arrived at Heathrow Airport and set down its passengers in the bus station. Saturday 23 November 2019.

The 234 was introduced as a replacement for the northern section of the 134 between Friern Barnet and Barnet Church in October 1989 with a mixed allocation of Metrobuses and Volvo Ailsas. This route has remained at Potters Bar Garage since but was demoted to single deck in 1994. In 1998, Metroline purchased the company MTL London Northern and this company still retains the route as demonstrated by DE1169 (PB) in Whetstone High Road. Saturday 30 November 2019.

Chapter 5

Tower Transit

Tower Transit is the company that was created when First London sold its London operations and apart from the number of routes and garages taken over by Stagecoach, Metroline, and Go-Ahead, this newly created company retained some routes/garages and has gained some routes in recent times. We look back to Monday 2 February 2009 when the whole of London and the South East awoke to a thick fall of snow and to make things worse, the whole bus network had been suspended until late into the evening peak, due to an incident involving a bendy bus. Northumberland Park's TN33127 (NP) lays over in the well-known Aldgate Bus Station surrounded by snow and slush and was the first bus that had been seen in service all morning at that point. Monday 2 February 2009.

The 58 was introduced in February 1960 between Walthamstow, Crooked Billet and Canning Town, replacing trolleybus route 685 under stage 5 of the trolleybus replacement programme and had peak extensions to both Silvertown on Saturdays and North Woolwich Monday to Friday using brand new shiny RMs at Walthamstow Garage and the old West Ham Garage. When West Ham Garage closed in 1992, it held the whole allocation which was transferred into Leyton Garage. In 1993, it was rerouted via Barking Road from Upton Park, Boleyn to East Ham, White Horse partially replacing the withdrawn 162. Today it runs between Walthamstow Central Station where it has terminated since 1988 and East Ham Central Park, the White Horse being dropped due to the pub being knocked down for redevelopment. Wednesday 15 June 2016. (*Terry Wong Min*)

Since the 1 April 2017, the 13 has been under the operation of Tower Transit. The route used to run between Golders Green and Aldwych, but it was withdrawn between Aldwych and Oxford Circus and diverted to Victoria Station replacing route 82 although, in reality, the 13 was withdrawn and the 82 simply renumbered as the 13. MV38214 (X) passes the famous Lords Cricket Ground named after Thomas Lord who founded it, this not being his original of three cricket grounds established between 1787 and 1814. His first ground stood in Dorset Square, and his second had to be abandoned to clear way for the construction of the Regent's Canal. Sunday 2 April 2017. (*Terry Wong Min*)

Route 69 operated between North Woolwich Free Ferry and Stratford when it was introduced in February 1960 as part replacement for trolleybus route 669 under stage 5 of the trolleybus replacement programme. In April 1960, it was extended to Chingford Mount under stage 6, replacing the 699. The route had a shared allocation between West Ham and Leyton Garages but in 1971, Poplar Garage received a brief Sunday allocation for a couple of months. In 1975, Walthamstow Garage received a share and after much coming and going of garage allocations, the route remained solely the share of Leyton until it was reallocated to the new West Ham Garage, the night element remaining at Leyton. The route was lost on tender in 2016 but due to the new buses not arriving, Stagecoach loaned the Tridents they operated the route with to Tower Transit until their buses arrived. DH38502 (LI) is one of three electric buses on the route and is seen at Canning Town Flyover. Saturday 5 May 2018.

This once very long and busy route was an east to west route right across Central London, running parallel to the Central Line between Stratford and Bond Street, where the route turned off Oxford Street down New Bond Street, via Berkeley Square and Green Park to Victoria. The section between Oxford Circus and Victoria was replaced by the 8 when that route was withdrawn from terminating at Willesden Garage and diverted to Victoria in 1992. VN36151 (LI) has just started its run to Ilford where before 1992 it would have continued to Becontree Heath. For a 25, this bus is very empty no doubt since the route no longer serves Oxford Street and is curtailed to finish at City Thameslink Station. Sunday 21 October 2018.

The original 23 ran from Becontree Heath to West London, paralleling the 15 between East Ham and Bank, but then continuing westwards via Cheapside and Holborn and rejoining the 15 at Oxford Circus. In January 1981, it was extended on weekdays, paralleling the 15 except for going via Tower Hill rather than Bank, to Oxford Circus. But less than three months later in April, it was withdrawn between Becontree and East Ham White Horse but extended at the western end to Ladbroke Grove alongside the 15 which it would later completely replace between Paddington and that point in 1992, when the route was reintroduced after being withdrawn in 1985. On the 30 September 2017, the route was curtailed to terminate at the Aldwych leaving the section beyond to Liverpool Street in the hands of the 11. On 24 November 2018, the 23 was withdrawn between Marble Arch and Aldwych and diverted to Hammersmith over the 10's routing from Marble Arch. Sunday 21 October 2018.

As part of Transport for London's Central London route changes, route RVI has now been withdrawn. Although this route does follow other routes at points along its journey, there were some roads previously unserved by buses along the Southbank area. This route crossed two bridges between Tower Gateway and Covent Garden, the historic Tower Bridge and Waterloo Bridge. The route was introduced in 2002 using Mercedes Benz Citaro and has seen some types come and go, including appearances by double deck types of the TN and VN class. The fleet used in its final years were these Hydrogen buses; WSH62997 (LI) stands next to the Novello Theatre, these have since swapped the City streets for more suburban roads of North East London on route 444, but these may be on borrowed time if they are withdrawn when the route goes to its new operator. Thursday 15 November 2018.

The 212 was introduced as a new route in 1981 between Chingford Station and the then open Walthamstow Garage where the route was allocated partly replacing routes 191 and the W21 using DMS types. These were later replaced by the more successful Leyland Titans until Capital Citybus and First ownership saw the route operated by a range of single and double deck types. CT Plus won the route from First in 2010 but it was won back by First's successor Tower Transit. Go-Ahead has since taken charge of the route in 2020. Its current routing began in 1988 between Chingford and St James Street stations, which are both on the same branch of London Overground out of Liverpool Street. Here we see VH38108 (LI) on the driver changeover stop just opposite Walthamstow Central Bus Station. Friday 14 December 2018.

In September 2011, The D8 was transferred from First to Go-Ahead and allocated to Silvertown Garage where it received new E200s, replacing First's DM Marshall bodied Dennis Darts. In November of that year, the route was extended in Stratford to terminate at the new Stratford City Bus Station, with a further extension in 2013 to Stratford International Station where it connects with the DLR, and Eurostar/South Eastern High Speed Line services. VN36158 (LI) departs Stratford. Friday 22 February 2019. (*Terry Wong Min*)

This was a new route introduced in December 1966 to replace the 26 between Leyton Bakers Arms and Victoria & Albert Docks; terminating at Stratford on Sundays it was allocated to Leyton Garage using RMLs. In 1968, the route was extended to Chingford Station where it served until curtailment at Walthamstow Central Station in 1973. In 1986, the eastern end of the route was projected to East Beckton District Centre and by 1988 the route no longer ventured further north than Stratford. In 1993, a new Savacentre superstore opened near to the A13 in Beckton and this saw an extension of the route along a piece of dual carriageway to terminate there, meeting the 325 and 366. In 1997, a new Showcase Cinema opened which saw a further small extension to terminate at the cinema, but this would later be cut back to Sainsbury's (former Savacentre) in 2008. This route was with Stagecoach for many years at Upton Park Garage. Monday 1 April 2019. (*Jimmy Sheng*)

The W15 has provided a route between Hackney Central and Walthamstow Central Stations since 1988, and once had minibuses operated by Lea Valley with their cream and green livery. When First took over the route from Arriva in 2012, new E200s were introduced to the route. These still work the route with Tower Transit. DML44281 (LI) is in Hoe Street, Walthamstow. Wednesday 11 December 2019.

Chapter 6

CT Plus

The 394 was introduced as a special service in 2001 with two minibuses between Dalston Market and Islington. In 2003, it became a proper addition to the London bus network and allocated eight Caetano Nimbus vehicles built on a Dennis Dart Chassis. DCS6 is seen in New North Road travelling to Homerton Hospital where it has served since 2003. Sunday 10 October 2010. *(Terry Wong Min)*

In 2003, CT Plus inaugurated new route 388 between Hackney Wick and Mansion House. The route got an extension along Queen Victoria Street in 2008 in order to aid the closure of Blackfriars Underground and National Rail Station for redevelopment works and saw a further extension to Temple followed by a final extension to Embankment Station. In 2013, it was extended eastwards to the new Stratford City Bus station via Eastway and the new Waterden Road. A projection beyond Blackfriars to Elephant & Castle for a period to replace a section of route 100 took place but in June 2019 was curtailed to Liverpool Street. A few months later in October, it saw another extension, this time replacing the 48 to London Bridge. 2529 (HK) is seen near Stratford International going to Blackfriars Station which was still its terminus until April 2017. Wednesday 15 March 2017. (*Terry Wong Min*)

The 26 replaced the eastern end of route 6 in 1992 between Hackney Wick and Aldwych where it diverges off across Waterloo Bridge to terminate at Waterloo Station; this route is exactly the same route as the 6A, withdrawn in 1968. The route was first operated by East London which was a subsidiary of London Buses, later taken over by Stagecoach under the tendering regime. History would repeat itself in 2006 when Stagecoach London sold its London bus operations to the Australian company Macquarie Bank. This resulted in the East London and Selkent names and logos being reintroduced to its East London and South East London vehicles. A five years reign with First/Tower Transit took place between 2011 and 2016 before its current operator CT Plus gained the route. 2501 (HK) is one of a batch of vehicles ordered for the 26, the HK garage code that is now carried by the route's vehicles indicates its operated by the CT Plus part of the shared Ash Grove Garage. Sunday 26 March 2017.

Introduced in 1993 between Bethnal Green Chest Hospital and Poplar Aberfeldy Estate, new midibus route 309 was tendered to Stagecoach East London and allocated to their Stratford Garage. In 1999, it saw an extension from Poplar to the new Canning Town Bus Station where it connected with the Jubilee Line, DLR and North London Line. OS27 (HK) has just passed under Canning Town Flyover and is a slightly larger dual door version of this usually single door make of vehicle. Saturday 5 May 2018.

The W19 replaced the Ilford to Walthamstow Central section of Thamesway route 551 which operated between Basildon and Walthamstow Central Monday to Saturday only, never venturing out of the Essex area on Sundays. This route has always been busy, even in its incarnation as the 551 on the Walthamstow Central-Ilford-Romford section especially on Saturdays where all three areas had markets. 1226 (AW) pulls off from the stop opposite Manor Park Station which will soon become a part of the long Elizabeth Line between Reading and Shenfield. Saturday 5 May 2019.

CT Plus has gained some routes in recent years, necessitating the building of a new garage in the Chingford area close to the old Walthamstow Dogs Stadium. The 20 was won from Go-Ahead London General in March 2019 but due to a few of the new buses not arriving in time, two E400s were loaned from Stagecoach to help keep the service going. 10114 is a Leyton bus and is seen here on the Debden Estate which is in the Epping Forest District of Essex constructed between 1947 and 1952. Tuesday 26 March 2019. (*Terry Wong Min*)

In 1989, Eastern National Citybus started operating new route W13 between Woodford Wells and Leytonstone Station. 1270 (HK) passes a statue of Sir Winston Churchill, who was once MP for Woodford Green, on its way to Leytonstone. Thursday 28 November 2019.

Route W12 was introduced between Wanstead and Walthamstow in 1988 and was allocated to Walthamstow Garage which was under London Forest ownership at the time. The route transferred to Thamesway in 1991 using Mercedes minibuses, which would later be replaced by more up to date vehicles in the late 1990s when First took over the service. In 2009, First took delivery of some new Optare Solos and when CT Plus took over the route in 2010, the same vehicle types were ordered. OS3 (AW) turns off down one of the side turnings along a hail and ride section of the route. Wednesday 11 December 2019.

Chapter 7

Abellio

In December 2009, a bus on the C3 overturned in Plough Road, Clapham when a lorry coming from a side turning carrying some railway tracks went into the side of the bus; the vehicle involved was 9823. Twenty people were injured including the driver with five of them having serious injuries. 9826 (QB) is a short wheelbase Dennis Trident seen at Clapham, these vehicles converted the route back in 2006 when they replaced single deck Optare Solos. Wednesday 26 June 2011. (*Terry Wong Min*)

A handful of London's buses use parts of dual carriageway and motorway on parts of their routes, allowing the bus to perform a bit of thrash that it wouldn't normally be able to do on a traffic-ridden high street, the 123, 173, and H91 are to name but a few. The K1 is another such route and 8122 (TF) has pulled off the A3 on its way into Kingston. Tuesday 17 June 2014. (*Terry Wong Min*)

London still has numerous prefix routes such as the 'C', 'D', 'R', 'U', and 'W' routes as well as numerous other letters. Transport for London brought in a policy towards the mid to late 2000s to renumber prefix routes without using letters. In the Addington area several 'T' routes were introduced when the Croydon Tramlink opened radiating off into various local areas connecting them with the trams, the buses wearing the same livery as the trams. The T33 was one of them and was renumbered to the 433 in October 2015, but the year before we see 8778 (BC) turning into Kingfisher Road in Selsdon. Monday 29 December 2014. (*Terry Wong Min*)

In 1951, the 188 was used to replace tram route 68 which only went as far as Waterloo, between Greenwich Cutty Sark and Chalk Farm Station, where it helped to supplement bus route 68, until cut back to Euston Station in 1970. In 1971, the route was converted to single deck SMSs, but these only lasted a few years when the route was converted to DMSs in 1976. Camberwell Leyland Titans took over in 1982 but in September of that year, DMSs returned with a New Cross allocation to the route until 1985. The route tendering regime in 1988 brought a motley collection of Leyland Atlanteans painted in a green and cream livery when Boro'line Maidstone were assigned the route contract. The 1990s would bring further colourful liveries with London & Country and Grey Green. Three years before, we saw Go-Ahead takeover the route Walworth's 9001 (WL) departs North Greenwich Bus Station for Russell Square where it has terminated since September 1999. Friday 7 November 2014.

The R68 was introduced between Hampton Court and Richmond in 1991, at the same time replacing the section of route 267 between Hampton Court and Fulwell Garage. Abellio took on this route in 2009 but prior to that, it was operated by its predecessor Travel London from 2005 until 2009 when that company became owned by Abellio. The driver of 8178 (TF) gives a friendly wave as he passes. Friday 27 October 2017. (*Terry Wong Min*)

The 68 used to ply between Chalk Farm Station and South Croydon Garage and had an allocation with Chalk Farm, Norwood, and South Croydon Garages with a Camberwell share in later years. In 1986, the route was withdrawn between Euston and Chalk Farm Station with that section covered by new route 168 but continued to serve Chalk Farm Station on Sundays only. 1994 saw the Euston to Chalk Farm Station as well as the Norwood Garage to South Croydon sections withdrawn and replaced by other routes. Between 2006 and 2018, this route was allocated to Camberwell Garage with Go-Ahead, however it literally moved over the road to Walworth Garage when Abellio took the contract in March 2018. LT694 (WL) approaches the roundabout around the Imax Cinema as it descends off Waterloo Bridge. Saturday 5 May 2018. (*Terry Wong Min*)

New route C10 appeared in 1991 using midibuses connecting Elephant & Castle and Victoria taking a rather indirect routing via Lambeth Bridge, Pimlico Station, and Buckingham Palace Road. In 2006, the route no longer served Lambeth Road and was rerouted to serve St Thomas's Hospital instead, where it picked up Lambeth Bridge via Lambeth Palace Road. It was also extended at the same time from Elephant & Castle via Borough, Bermondsey, Jamaica Road, and Rotherhithe Station to terminate at Canada Water Bus Station. Abellio gained this route from Go-Ahead London in 2011 and received new E200's like Walworth's 8863 (WL) seen on Westminster Bridge Road. Sunday 6 May 2018. (*Terry Wong Min*)

Stockley Park sits in the Harlington area in the London Borough of Hillingdon. The site of the business park that is situated here was once a tip where business and industrial waste from the West London area would be offloaded from barges. Some well-known companies have premises here today including Canon, Marks & Spencer and Apple Inc. 9462 (WS) is seen on the U5 which terminates at the business park, heading for Uxbridge. Saturday 30 June 2018. (*Terry Wong Min*)

Newly introduced on 2 December 2006 between Wandsworth Road Station and Kensal Rise Station, the 452 took up service using Travel London Dennis Tridents before it started to see E400s introduced in 2007 which eventually replaced them. An extension to the route from Wandsworth Road Station to terminate at Vauxhall Bus Station took place in November 2016. Tower Transit won this route in 2018, operated out of Westbourne Park Garage; however, a month or so before the takeover we see the route still in the hands of Abellio with 9417 (QB) about to swing round in Ladbroke Grove Sainsbury's. Sunday 21 October 2018.

Under stage 8 of the trolleybus replacement programme, the 207 replaced the 607 trolleybus which previously replace the 7 tram between Uxbridge and Shepherds Bush Green in November 1960. A short extension to the route from Shepherds Bush Green round to White City Bus Station took effect from November 2008, via a new road built alongside the West London Line incorporating some of the old Wood Lane Depot Central Line car sheds that were retained. This route would become famous (or not) when it was the last route to operate bendy buses on the night of 9 December 2011. At Ealing Common, 9529 (GW) heads east for White City; this route no longer terminates at Uxbridge. Saturday 20 April 2019.

When the 414 was introduced in 2002 as a new route, it provided a useful connection from the Fulham and Kensington areas to Maida Vale via Knightsbridge, Park Lane and the Edgware Road operated by First London. Originally terminating at Fulham High Street, a better terminus was sought at Putney Bridge Station when it was extended there in 2003. In 2009, the contract was given to Abellio London who have managed to maintain this route after getting a contract renewal in 2014. 9526 (QB) pulls out of Park Lane about to round Marble Arch. Bank Holiday Monday 26 August 2019.

The northern terminus of the 109 used to serve Westminster Bridge-Victoria Embankment-Blackfriars Bridge in a clockwise and anti-clockwise loop, in the same format as tram routes 16 and 18 used to operate that this route replaced back in 1951. The route was converted to OPO in 1987 and the loop abandoned to terminate at Trafalgar Square instead. The 109 served Purley for many years at its southern end until its OPO conversion in 1987 and was a replacement for Sunday route 59. Brixton, Streatham, Thornton Heath, and South Croydon Garages have shared the allocation over the years but towards the end, before Abellio gained this route from Arriva, it was allocated to Brixton. 9488 (BC) passes through Brixton and is about to make its ascent up Brixton Hill towards Streatham. Thursday 25 July 2019.

The H28 must be a very long and boring route enough to send a passenger to sleep on this bus! Hounslow has a collection of 'H' routes orbiting off the bus station some of which have replaced the tail ends of old trunk routes. The H28 was a new route introduced to the Hounslow area in 1995 using London & Country midibuses between Osterley and Hounslow Garage. 1995 saw an extension at both ends first to Osterley Tesco then at the other end to Bulls Bridge Tesco where the route still runs today. Travel London gained this route in 2005 from Telling's Golden Miller and the route has been retained through into the Abellio era seen by 8585 (TF), turning into a side road in Cranford. Sunday 8 September 2019.

Introduced in November 1997 and awarded to Epsom Buses between Sutton and Roundshaw, the S4 saw an extension beyond Sutton to Morden Station in 1998. Quality Line had a run of the route from 2007 to 2014 when Abellio took over and brought slightly better buses than the Optare Solos used by Quality Line in the shape of E200s. 8203 (BC) is seen on the Roundshaw Estate where it shares the road with the 154 and 455. It is weird seeing the emergency door positioned in the middle of the body, as opposed to before the last rear offside window where it has been situated for so many years on OPO buses. Many London builds have been built without one at all. Friday 18 October 2019.

The E9 began its life in 1990 using Renault Reeve Burgess minibuses with Ealing Buses branding on the side. The route was allocated to Hanwell Garage, but this garage closed in 1993 and the route moved into Greenford. It is hard to imagine how people would manage without a bus service on a Saturday or Sunday today; this route only received its Sunday operation in 2001. This route, buses, and Greenford Garage transferred over to Metroline in 2013 but they would give way to Abellio in 2016 when the route was won under tender which also included conversion of the route to double deck for the first time in its existence. 9531 (GW) is seen in Yeading Lane. Sunday 9 December 2019. (*Terry Wong Min*)

Chapter 8

London United

The H91 was introduced in 1991 between Hammersmith and Hounslow West Station replacing part of the old route 91, which until the point it was withdrawn operated between Wandsworth Bridge and Hounslow West Station. DPS674 (HH) was once part of a large fleet of Plaxton Pointer bodied Dennis Darts which both Hounslow and Hounslow Heath Garages had allocated to most of their routes. All of these would be replaced by new E200s or double deck vehicles when some of the routes converted to double deck. This route did convert to double deck in 2009 using Scania Omnicities; these gave way as part of a low emission scheme along Chiswick High Road to hybrid vehicles. Sunday 25 October 2009.

In 1941, the 214 was renumbered to 131 and converted from single to double deck operation operating between Kingston Bus Station and Walton-on-Thames using STs allocated to Kingston Garage. In 1949, it received its allocation of RTs and in 1952 moved over to Norbiton Garage; both garages closed many years ago. This route has had a number of interesting extensions over the years, travelling deep into the Surrey countryside to towns such as Weybridge, Hersham and West Molesley. The route's northern termini has also been interesting besides terminating at Wimbledon for most of its time, it has ventured beyond to Clapham Common on Sundays, with morning journeys on that day of the week to Aldwych taking place in 1984 and 1985. TA220 (FW) was once part of a batch of Tridents allocated to the route, these were replaced by Scania Omnicities now replaced themselves by Volvo hybrids. Saturday 21 August 2011. (*Terry Wong Min*)

A rarity on the 49, TLA27 (S) has escaped onto the route when seen loading up at Shepherds Bush Station. The coming of the Westfields Shopping Centre in Shepherds Bush created better interchange facilities between buses, and the newly rebuilt Central Line and London Overground stations. TLA27 formed a batch of Dennis Tridents delivered for Routemaster replacement on the 94 in January 2004; after new hybrid E400s ousted them in 2010, they were allocated to the 220, with some later being dispersed further south west to garages such as Hounslow and Fulwell. Sunday 28 October 2012. (*Terry Wong Min*)

Remembrance Day 2013 sees LT72 (V) standing in Hammersmith Bus Station, built in 1993 in conjunction with the rebuilding of Hammersmith Underground Station serving the District and Piccadilly Lines. The number 9 is one of London's oldest routes and in the 1930s reached as far east as Romford and Rainham. For many years, the route was crewed by Barking, Dalston, and Mortlake crews with a Sunday round trip between Mortlake and Becontree Heath said to have taken three hours one way. Sunday operations would also be very interesting in the 1990s where we would see OPO buses being used by Hounslow, Stamford Brook, and Shepherds Bush including some single deck Dennis Darts which would be unthinkable today on a busy Central London route. Route 9 would be the third LT route of 2013 to be converted back to crew operation as can be seen with its rear open platform on this LT. Monday 11 November 2013.

The 142 was introduced in 1914 by the London General Omnibus Company. This route crosses the Greater London Boundary at its northern end serving Watford Junction; its southern terminus is Brent Cross Shopping Centre which it has served since 1976 when it opened but prior to 1970, the route continued beyond here down the Edgware Road to terminate at Kilburn Park Station. RATP Soverign won the route tender a few weeks previous to this shot, introducing hybrid vehicles to the route like ADE40403 (BT), seen in Stanmore in very idyllic settings. Tuesday 30 January 2018. (*Terry Wong Min*)

By the time route 18 was used to replace the 662 trolleybus between Paddington Green and Sudbury, it was already a well-established North West London route between Edgware and London Bridge Stations, with Monday to Friday peak hour journeys serving London Transports Aldenham Overhaul Works in Aldenham. The route has run between Sudbury and Euston since October 1995. In 2003, this route was converted to bendy bus operation but come the contract renewal in 2010, the route gained back its double deckers. VH45235 (PR) is seen on the first day of London United ownership. Friday 17 November 2017. (*Terry Wong Min*)

London is not a stranger to the Mercedes Citaro, but the shorter version depicted here is not usually the choice of the other operators who have some in their fleets. MCS08 (EB) is seen on the 413 in Lower Morden, a route newly introduced in 1990 replacing a part of the 213; in 1991 it was extended between Sutton to Lower Morden replacing a part of the 151. These Citaro look like they are slightly smaller than the LDPs they replaced. Monday 26 December 2016. (*Terry Wong Min*)

The K4 was introduced in 1989 and was awarded to Westlink where it was allocated to Kingston Garage. The route was transferred to Tolworth in 2001, where it is still allocated today. SDE20297 (TV) is seen on its trip to Kingston with St Mark's Church as its backdrop setting. Saturday 28 July 2018. (*Terry Wong Min*)

Route 288 was introduced in June 1972 using a single SMS vehicle operating in a circular route starting at Edgware station and ending back at Edgware Station. This route would see a gradual increase in vehicles and a more point to point route created. At the start of privatisation, Metroline would take control of the route and garage at Edgware. The route saw a decade of double deck Metrobus operation before going back to single. September 2018 saw the route won from Arriva Shires who operated the route out of the now closed Garston Garage and awarded to London Sovereign, whose new DLE30257 (BT) is seen down Edgwarebury Road on its way to Queensbury Morrison's. Sunday 7 October 2018.

This incarnation of the route number 70 started in 1991 as a Gold Arrow midibus route operating out of Westbourne Park Garage. For some years, the route has plied between Acton and South Kensington Station, gradually getting larger single deck Darts. Several bus operating companies have had a run of the route from Thorpes, Metroline, First London (later Tower Transit), before it was won on tender by London United in 2017. At Ladbroke Grove Sainsbury's, Shepherds Bush, BE37007 (S) gleams in the sun on its way to Chiswick Business Park which was built on the site of the former London Transport Chiswick Works. After much deferment, this route was finally extended to Chiswick Business Park on 30 January 2016. Sunday 21 October 2019.

The H17 was introduced in 1989 as a new two bus route between Harrow Bus Station and Sudbury Vale Farm Sports Centre operated by R&I Coaches who had a base in the Park Royal area. Sovereign took over from R&I and would later be absorbed into the London United company. DEs replaced the old Plaxton Pointer Dennis Darts in 2011 and like all the buses in London United's fleet (except the LT class) have been renumbered into new longer fleet numbers as worn by DE20179 (RP). Saturday 17 November 2018.

The two-door version of the LT (NBfL) has not really been ordered in large numbers, with batches ordered by London Sovereign for the 183 and Go-Ahead for the 37. London Sovereign have classed them as VHRs and VHR45203 (SO) finds itself onto another Harrow route the H14. Saturday 17 November 2018.

Route 10 was an East London area route until January 1988, when the route and number were withdrawn. Seven months later, the route number reappeared into circulation as a route operating between King's Cross and Hammersmith, replacing the 73 between Hyde Park Corner and Hammersmith. Holloway Garage gradually gained the whole allocation and the route extended to Archway all day daily. This route was chopped in half in 2003, the King's Cross to Hammersmith section operated by First using OPO buses, the Routemasters from the 10 being allocated to newly created crew route 390 which operated between Archway and Marble Arch. LT61 (V) in its Poppy Appeal ad sits on the stand in York Way in the last week the route would exist as again the route and number have since been withdrawn. Thursday 22 November 2018.

Another special livery bus is Tolworth's SP40102 (TV) seen leaving Kingston on the 71. Before TfL's all red rule was enforced, London United's buses were adorned in this livery, giving much relief from the boring all-over red. The 71 has terminated at Chessington since 1980, when it served the then Chessington Zoo which is now Chessington World of Adventures theme park. London United have kept this route since 1989. Tuesday 23 July 2019. (*Terry Wong Min*)

London United took over Epsom Coaches in 2017 after they ceased trading and their operations were incorporated into RATP London United's operations. Taken at Tolworth Station, ADE40310 (EB) shows off its Quality Line RATP Group logos that have now been applied and it has been renumbered into London United's longer fleet numbering system. During Race Days at Epsom, a special bus service numbered 406F is provided to shuttle racegoers between the train station and racecourse; many years ago this route would see any bus available from any garage turn up to help on the service. Tuesday 26 March 2019. (*Terry Wong Min*)

Between 1982 and 1991, the 27 operated between Archway and Richmond before it saw curtailments to both its northern and southern ends with the Camden Town to Archway section replaced by new route 135 (Archway to Marble Arch) and the Turnham Green to Richmond section by new route 391 (Richmond To Fulham Broadway). In 1995, it was extended up Camden High Street to terminate at the Chalk Farm Safeway store. In 2012, after much delay, the western end was extended to Chiswick Business Park, but this would only last a few years as the route has been cut back to Hammersmith (Hammersmith & City and Circle Lines) Station in March 2019. This route has recently been awarded to Abellio in November 2019 but back in the summer, LT92 (V) is seen still in the hands of London United in Camden Gardens. Sunday 25 August 2019.

The 272 was introduced in 2002, replacing part of route H40 and awarded to London United. Between 2007 and 2009, the route briefly went away from London United to a company called NCP Challenger who had a handful of other South West London routes including the 33. In May 2019, London United got a contract renewal for this route which included the ordering of new buses. DME30379 (V) stops opposite Turnham Green. Sunday 8 September 2019.

Hounslow route 203 was new in February 1951, between Hanworth and Hounslow Central Station. Apart from its stint with Westlink, London Buslines, Telling's Golden Miller, and Travel London, this route has remained at Hounslow Garage from 1951 to 1986, then again from 2006 to time of writing in December 2019. Mercedes Citaro are the order of the day when seen here with MCL30304 (AV) on the approach to Hounslow West Station. This route still serves between Hounslow and Staines just as it did in the 1960s. Sunday 8 September 2019.

Seen on the second day of its new contract with a new operator, the 395 runs between Harrow-on-the-Hill Bus Station and Greenford Westway Cross where it serves a retail Park, serving some back streets along the way. DE20199 (SO) pulls off from a stop along Cheltenham Close, Northolt. A few years ago, this section would probably have been 'hail and ride' but many routes that travel down residential streets seem to be getting fixed stops placed on the route now, the 300 being another such route where this has happened. This route replaced the 398 between Northolt and Greenford. Sunday 8 September 2019.

The H11 formed one of the group of routes that were operated under the Harrow Buses umbrella, replacing a part of route 183 between Pinner and Northwood in 1987. Sovereign took over the contract from December 1990, which also saw an extension from Harrow-on-the-Hill to nearby Northwick Park Hospital. Sovereign was purchased by London United in 2002 and now trades as London Sovereign, DLE30282 (SO) is seen in Porlock Avenue, South Harrow. The RATP Group is a French state-owned public transport operator. Sunday 8 September 2019.

With the odd deviances to the route, the 183 has served the same Golders Green to Pinner routing since 1934 when it commenced operation allocated to Hendon Garage. The old Hendon Garage was the main provider between 1942 until 1987 when Hendon closed, and the route transferred into Harrow Weald. SP40076 (SO) has just started out on its journey having just passed beneath the Metropolitan and Chiltern Railway Lines at Pinner. Sunday 8 September 2019.

Between 1971 and 1992, the 105 provided a connection from Shepherds Bush Green to Heathrow Airport, with the section between Shepherds Bush and Southall being renumbered as the 95 on Monday to Saturdays. In 1995, this route was converted to minibus operation; however, a change of operator to London & Country in 1996 saw bigger single deck vehicles introduced with route branding added to the buses. Ten years later, the upper deck was restored when First took over the contract using TN class buses. London United gained this route from Metroline in June 2018 using these new VHs. A very big gap in the service this day sees VH45273 (HH) only going as far as Harlington Corner crossing the M4 Motorway in Southall Lane. Sunday 8 September 2019.

The H37 was introduced in May 1991 to replace the Richmond to Hounslow section of long trunk route 37 which was curtailed at Putney High Street and partly replaced by the 337. The 1980s and '90s were an interesting time for vehicle allocations with the route starting off with new DT Dennis Darts; the allocation would see two Leyland Nationals followed by two Leyland Lynx added, with Leyland Nationals taking over the full allocation in 1996. DXE30353 (AV) heads into Hounslow through Isleworth. Sunday 8 September 2019.

The 267 was introduced on the 9 May 1962, replacing the 667 trolleybus between Hammersmith and Hampton Court Station in the final stage 14 of London's trolleybus replacement programme at Fulwell Garage, which ironically started London's first trolleybus routes in 1931. In 1991, the section between Fulwell Bus Garage and Hampton Court Station was withdrawn and replaced by new route R68, the following year, a summer extension over its withdrawn routing was introduced between May and October and this lasted until September 2011 when it was stopped completely. When the 267 was converted to LTs from 2017, it was allocated the very last LT built LT1000, which has since transferred to Abellio who has recently gained the route in November 2019. LT990 (FW) is seen in Twickenham Road two months before the route went over. Sunday 8 September 2019.

The S1 was introduced as a midibus route in 1993 between Beddington Corner and Sutton Station and awarded to London & Country with their distinctive green livery. London General won the route in 1996 before it came to Quality Line. In 2014, it was rerouted and extended to serve Lavender Fields where SDE20289 (EB) is seen heading for in Middleton Road, Mitcham. Friday 18 October 2019.

This route has been a success story from the word go when it was introduced as part of the new Congestion Charge introduced by Transport for London to try and help reduce congestion in the Central London area, operating to a west to south axis between Shepherds Bush Green and Camberwell Green via the Bayswater Road, Park Lane, Victoria Street, Westminster Bridge Road, and Walworth Road. In 2008, the route saw a small extension to the new White City Bus Station and in the same year was used to trial out some Optare Olympus buses classed as SOs for a period in 2008 but these were displaced in 2009 when the route received new SPs. In 2014, OPO LTs replaced the SPs on this route and they are still operating today. LT141 (S) is seen in Bressenden Place, Victoria. Wednesday 13 November 2019.

Shepherds Bush Poppy bus VH45189 (S) is seen turning into Bath Road at Turnham Green Station looking resplendent in the late autumn sunshine. These vehicles replaced earlier E400 hybrid vehicles. The section of this route between Oxford Circus and Acton Green was originally part of the long 88 route between Clapham Common and Acton Green, and was created in 1990, operating between Oxford Circus and Acton Green as a crew route, being OPO on Sundays terminating at Trafalgar Square. In 2001, the route settled down to operate between Acton Green and Piccadilly Circus where the buses stood in Charles II Street as they do today. This route gets slaughtered when the Central Line goes down paralleling it between Oxford Circus and Shepherds Bush, even more so now the 390 no longer goes up to Notting Hill Gate! Saturday 16 November 2019.

Introduced in 1971, the 258 was a replacement route for the 182 between Watford Junction and Harrow-on-the-Hill Station using MBs allocated to Harrow Weald Garage. These were replaced by SMS vehicles in 1978, which lasted until Leyland Nationals took over in 1979, with a Saturday allocation using all Metrobuses. In 1996, the route saw the yellow and brown livery of London Buslines, followed by First Centre West, and Arriva London North although being allocated to Garston Garage which was previously an Arriva Shires garage. London Sovereign gained this route in 2017, ADE40409 (BT) makes a stop at Harrow & Wealdstone Station. Saturday 23 November 2019.

The 111 today operates a long route between Heathrow Central and Kingston going the long way via Cranford, Heston, Hounslow, Whitton, and Hanworth, passing the historic Hampton Court Palace before getting into Kingston. Hampton Court Palace was built in the sixteenth century and was often a place of residence for Henry VIII who brought all six of his wives here some of them before they unfortunately lost their heads at the Tower. It first became a tourist attraction in 1838 when Queen Victoria opened it to the public and it still attracts millions of tourists to this day and is even said to have some famous ghosts haunting its buildings and grounds. Hounslow's SP40178 (AV) has just set down its passengers at the last stop at Heathrow Airport Central Bus Station. Saturday 23 November 2019.

Chapter 9

Sullivan Bus

Most of London's bus operators operate school routes that have been contracted by TfL. Some of the routes operate over sections of more than one normal service route, providing up to two journeys in one or both directions, to help stop normal service buses getting swamped by school children, although many continue to take the normal bus routes also. The 626 is one example seen operated by ALX6 (SM) former Stagecoach London 17548 seen in Ballards Lane, Finchley. Monday 20 April 2015. *(Terry Wong Min)*

The 298 was introduced in 1968 as part replacement for two of the 29 family routes replacing the 29 between Southgate and Clare Hall Hospital/Borehamwood and the full length of the 29B which operated between Potters Bar and Turnpike Lane Station. Between 1970-73 and 1975-77, the route saw extensions beyond Turnpike Lane Station to Finsbury Park but each time it would revert to terminating at Turnpike Lane Station. The deregulation in 1986 saw London Country North East take control of the route, followed by Grey Green, and First Capital Citybus. In February 2012, Sullivan Bus was awarded the contract from Arriva using E200s, which the route is still allocated, but occasionally double deckers appear like DS54 (SM) which is an ex Stagecoach London Scania Omnicity terminating at Arnos Grove Station. Sunday 26 May 2019. (*Jimmy Sheng*)

A new minibus route introduced in 1972, this was another route to receive the FS class. The W9 would later see operation in the privatisation era by Eastern National Citybus and Thamesway with their colourful liveries, as well as First Capital's red and yellow buses. Sullivan Bus would be successful with their bid for the route, winning it from Metroline in 2017. AE26 (SM) departs from the Art Deco Southgate Station built in 1932 for the Piccadilly Line Cockfosters Extension. Much of the housing developments of this area sprang up as a result of the Underground being extended through here. Monday 5 June 2017. (*Terry Wong Min*)

As well as operating the 299, Sullivan Bus also operate the 399 which, when it began in 1993, operated in a circular route starting and finishing at Barnet General Hospital via Great North Road, Cockfosters Road, Hadley Wood Station, and Barnet High Street serving some back streets. SL94 (SM) passes Hadley Wood Station. Saturday 20 October 2018. (*Terry Wong Min*)

Although the 306 is not a TfL area route as such, it is worth mentioning here as it is operated by Sullivan Buses who are back into the London market of operating routes, and the 306 certainly serves the old area of London Transport/London Country and connects with some London routes. The other reason is that the company has painted their E200 Darts for the route in this attractive green with yellow waist relief band which resembles the livery worn by vehicles owned by London Country. AE6 (SM) swings into the bus station at Elstree & Borehamwood Station bound for North Borehamwood. Saturday 24 August 2019.

The 217 used to serve beyond Waltham Cross Bus Station where it terminates today when it used to go via Waltham Abbey to terminate at Upshire which are both districts of Epping Forest in Essex, but in 1982, that section was replaced by a new route, 250A. The routing was simply a renumbering of the 144A in 1954 and was allocated to both Enfield and West Green Garages; upon the closure of the latter in 1962 it moved into nearby Wood Green. In 1998, the route was operated by single deckers, but the upper deck returned in 2003 at the start of the new contract. This route shares the road between Turnpike Lane Station and Southbury Road with the 231, E75 (SM) is one of the batches of vehicles delivered to take up the service back in June 2016 and is seen traversing the Roundway, West Arm in Tottenham. Tuesday 27 August 2019. (*Terry Wong Min*)

Chapter 10

Heritage Routes

Heritage routes 9 and 15 both started service on Monday 14 November 2005, 26 days before the last ever crew operated route 159 ceremoniously saw off its last Routemasters into the history books. Before the first buses travelled in service along the route, a press launch took place at Trafalgar Square where the then Mayor Ken Livingston was present to launch the service, and perhaps try and win back some popularity with Londoners. Here we see RM1776 (X) on the Kensington Road approaching the Royal Albert Hall which was the route's terminus for the first five years. Bank Holiday Monday 31 August 2009.

Also on the same day and location, we see RM1913 (X) pulling out of Exhibition Road on its way back to the Aldwych. On arriving at the Royal Albert Hall, the route made a loop around the Royal Albert Hall via Queens Gate, turning into Prince Consort where it had a bus stand. Departing for Aldwych the buses would turn out of Prince Consort into Exhibition Road then right back into Kensington Road where the first pick up stop would be at Prince of Wales Gate. This wasn't a good set up for people wanting to travel back from the Royal Albert Hall on a 9H and the route's extension to Kensington High Street would see a better traffic objective achieved. Bank Holiday Monday 31 August 2009.

As mentioned on the previous page, Heritage route 9 was extended at its western end from the Royal Albert Hall to Kensington High Street but at the same time cut back from the Aldwych to terminate at Trafalgar Square. SRM3 (RM1650) (X) stands at the Kensington High Street stand close to Addison Road. Here it displays some different colour roundels in a display reminiscent of the Olympic Rings, but these would not last long, being taken off almost straight away which was a shame as it was a good artistic idea and helped promote the 2012 Olympics. The silver livery and white stripe with the UK flag however remained intact. Monday 11 November 2011.

The amended livery SRM3 (RM1650) (X) received without the Roundels forming the Olympic Rings. Approaching the Royal Albert Hall. Monday 12 March 2012. (*Terry Wong Min*)

Both Stagecoach and First (later Tower Transit) had some very enthusiastic staff both on the operational/managerial side and behind the scenes and thanks to them buses were turned out in different liveries like the white roundel and relief band, and the 1933 livery on RM1933 that was on the 15H. First/Tower Transit also had some oddities to the traditional London Transport livery originally applied to the fleets such as RM1562 (X) seen here at Green Park, Constitution Hill with a gold relief band, London Transport and First decals. RM1562 became a part of the LT Museum collection when it was purchased in 1998, however it was bought back by TfL to be refurbished by Marshall's to become part of the dedicated fleet for route 13. Saturday 5 May 2012.

Back in 2012, the 9H and the normal route 9 were both rerouted away from Lower Regent Street, Haymarket, Piccadilly, and Piccadilly Circus to serve Pall Mall and St James Street where the route would join its original routing between Green Park Station and Trafalgar Square. RM1627 (X) looks immaculate as it passes St James Palace on its way to Kensington High Street. Note the silver tape applied to the front upper deck windows by an enthusiastic driver on the route, making it to look as though it has its original quarter drop wind down windows again, a very nice touch compared to the other fixed sealed windows. The normal route 9 has since been put back to its routing via Piccadilly Circus and Piccadilly. Bank Holiday Monday 5 May 2014.

Old and new. RM1776 (X) leads 'New Routemaster' LT83 (V) around Hyde Park Corner and into Piccadilly on its way to Trafalgar Square. The 9H originally used to go through to Aldwych, but was later cut back to Trafalgar Square and extended at its western end from the Royal Albert Hall to High Street Kensington as a better traffic objective to increase passenger patronage on the route, but the frequency decreased from every 15 minutes to every 20 minutes using only four buses. Bank Holiday Monday 5 May 2014.

Come In Number Nine, Your Time Is Up. In 2014, it was decided that statistics showed that the Heritage 9 was not earning enough money due to low patronage, although the crews who worked it and passengers that used it regularly would have argued differently. The last day had come and RM1627 (X) performed the last rites and even adorned a specially made blind for its via box to tell everyone of the occasion. Seen in Pall Mall, it nears its very last trip to Trafalgar Square. The final journey was full of enthusiasts and included a very lively photo stop at the last stop in Kensington. Friday 25 July 2014.

After the final journey, staff at the garage arranged for photos to be taken at Westbourne Park where buses were lined up and different blind displays put up for photos. After everyone got their photos, the buses have been parked up awaiting their futures with RM1562, RM1776, and RM1913 on the left, and SRM3 which has been retained by Tower Transit for special events etc. Friday 25 July 2014.

A freshly repainted RM1941 (BW) shows off its gleaming paintwork as it sits inside Bow Garage; it is yet to receive its white relief band to match its white fleet numbers and solid roundels. It also adorns some London Pride posters; this brand of beer was introduced in 1959, and takes its name from a flower that grew on the bomb sites during the London Blitz which was said to have boost the morale of Londoners who, despite getting bombed night after night, held on to hope by seeing this flower grow amongst the carnage and ruins. Sunday 29 June 2008.

From time to time, special events have prevented the 15H from running part of or the full route. Thanks to the then General Manager, the RMs could be found operating at either the eastern or western end of the normal route 15, which at the time the western end still terminated at Paddington Station (with a brief extension round to Paddington Basin). Here we see RM871 (WH) leading RM1941 (WH) working from Paddington without its adverts into Regent Street where it will pick up its line of route from Trafalgar Square to Tower Hill. The new crossing at Oxford Circus can be seen here and has made crossing this big junction a lot easier. Monday 31 May 2010.

At the Tower Hill end of the route, the 15H stands on a designated bus stand in Minories around the corner from Tower Gateway DLR Station. RML2760 (WH) was a long-time performer on the normal 15 before the route converted to OPO on 31 August 2003, when it performed the last rites being the last bus back to East Ham, White Horse and into Upton Park Garage. During the Olympic Games, this special vinyl advert was applied but the bus never operated on the heritage route with this applied. In the early years of the heritage route, both RML2760 and RML2665 made regular appearances amongst the RMs and were the choice to wait for with their wind down windows and original (RML2760) and near original (RML2665) engines. Here it is seen on the stand working as a staff taxi from the garage; the driver kindly posed it with the 15H blinds up. Saturday 21 August 2010.

Another occasion saw a special operation between Aldgate and Limehouse, Burdett Road. RM1968 (WH) turns out of Burdett Road into Commercial Road on its way to Aldgate. This bus's red livery, white band, and solid white roundel was worn on most London buses and red Underground trains between 1974 and the mid-to-late-1980s given the name 'GLC Livery'. It is thought that this livery gave a fresh modern look, especially to the Routemaster bus; some readers may argue the traditional London Transport Red livery with gold band and underlined fleet name and numbers are better. Once TfL started to get some of the heritage Routemasters refurbished to near original condition, the three buses painted into this livery received the traditional LT livery again. Sunday 5 September 2010.

The London City skyline has had a long period of change as older buildings from the 1960s that replaced the bomb damaged buildings during the London Blitz are themselves being replaced. As RM1933 (WH) leaves Cannon Street across the junction of Queen Victoria Street at the Mansion House, we see above some of the new buildings and cranes working on another. This livery was the third applied to RM1933 recreating when it was painted into London Transport 1933 livery back in 1983, to celebrate London Transport's Golden Jubilee whilst it was based at Chalk Farm Garage (CF) for the 24, 31, and 68. Bank Holiday Monday 5 May 2014.

Today, the 15H is the only remaining route out of the two and on 2 March 2019, the route which ran seven days a week except Christmas Day was reduced to operate Summer weekends, and Bank Holidays only. Here we see West Ham's rather down-at-heel-looking RM2050 (WH) basking in the sunshine at St Paul's Churchyard which has seen much change, there now being gardens either side for people to sit, the garden seen here sitting on top of the old coach park area. Sunday 26 March 2017.

Chapter 11

Tour Bus Routes

One regular tour in Central London and along the Thames but no longer operating was the Duck Tour, which visited various tourist attractions in the Central London area such as Westminster and Trafalgar Square, finishing with a ride in the River Thames gaining access at a ramp next to the MI5 building in Vauxhall. Unfortunately, several engine fires whilst in service saw the vehicles and the tour withdrawn completely. These historic vehicles date back to the D-Day operation of 1944 in Normandy, France where they were used to transport many British soldiers onto the beaches to help fight back the Nazi war machine. Considering how old the vehicles were, they had a good innings. Here *Mistress Quickly* roars towards Hyde Park Corner. Friday 4 May 2012.

An operation started up in London, as well as York and Edinburgh, is the Ghost Bus Tour, visiting various locations that are said to be haunted in those cities. Here RM1101 is seen at the Bank about to turn into King William Street heading towards London Bridge. Many Routemasters lost their cherished registration numbers upon being sold after service in London, this being one of them reregistered KFF 367. Wednesday 12 March 2014.

This London Bus Experience tour bus looks like it has a good load up top as well as a number downstairs in the form of RM1979 in Pall Mall. This bus had a long association with Metroline and predecessor MTL London with stints on the newest route to be introduced at the time with RMs, the 139 as well as at Willesden Garage on the 6 and 98. This bus thankfully kept its original registration number. Bank Holiday Monday 5 May 2014.

The Big Bus Tour was started in London in 1991 and over the years has become a success story expanding to countries all over the world including Malta, China, Hong Kong, Dubai, America, and numerous other places. Here DA227 is working the Eastbound Red route at St Pauls Churchyard and was one of a small batch of open top E400s bought to replace some of the older tri-axle vehicles. Sunday 26 March 2019.

Golden Tours is a coach operating company but broke into the open top tour bus market in London in 2011 using some recently withdrawn Stagecoach London Dennis Tridents. As emissions regulations have now become stricter in Central London, newer buses were ordered to replace the tridents in the form of this Volvo Evoseti on the stand at Hyde Park Corner in this attractive livery on the Red Route. Sunday 3 June 2018.

Also at the Hyde Park Corner stand is former Metroline VPL162 which was recently withdrawn from Holloway Garage, and is performing lighter duties than when it worked arduous routes such as the 4, 43, and 390, as well as some other Holloway routes. It has also gained the name *Julia*. City Tour London is a subsidiary group of Ensignbus who used to operate tour buses in London back in the 1980s and '90s. Sunday 3 June 2019.

Brigit's Afternoon Tea Tour Bus is another new tour that has popped up using a Routemaster that was decked out specially inside with two seats facing each other and a table, where the passengers of the tour are served tea and cream scones whilst taking in the sights of London. As this tour's patronage has grown, so has its fleet including ex-heritage route 9 RM1204. RM1790 leads RML2404 on one of the departures past the cenotaph in Whitehall. Sunday 3 June 2018.

Stagecoach introduced three new Mega Sightseeing Tour routes back in 2018. Initially introduced with converted Dennis Tridents, due to further changes in emissions regulations these were replaced with newer E400s displaced from Bromley Garage. The route is based and controlled from Bow Garage, 19133 (BW) is seen in Tooley Street opposite London Bridge Station. Thursday 6 June 2019. (*Terry Wong Min*)

The Classic Tour is a small tour using open top RM1398 that has three departures from Northumberland Avenue in the afternoon taking tourists on a 75 minutes tour, via the City, Westminster Abbey, and Buckingham Palace. The tour also serves The London Eye, Tower of London, The Shard, and St Paul's Cathedral on weekends only. The bus is seen entering Parliament Square. Thursday 8 August 2019.

Chapter 12

Driver Training, Service Vehicles and Dial a Ride Vehicles

For some time after Arriva withdrew their Metrobuses from service, several were kept as driver trainers. Each morning, two vehicles would be seen making their way northwards to Stamford Hill Garage. M1130 was one of those two buses seen swinging into Egerton Road, Stamford Hill still carrying its red livery, the second vehicle carried a white trainer livery which on later training vehicles would turn to turquoise as seen in the chapter title page picture. This picture was taken in the last week of the use of Metrobuses on trainer duties. Wednesday 25 June 2008.

The 101 received these Wright Scania early Low Floor wheelchair accessible buses and given the class coding SLW. They also had an early form of ibus with audio announcements and display screens that told passengers the next stop and bus stopping, but these later fell into disuse. The last examples were withdrawn in 2005 when route 101's contract renewal included new buses and conversion to double deck with new Dennis Tridents taking over. 28616 (BW) is seen allocated to Bow where it is seen parked at the back, it has been given a fresh coat of paint as well as East London logos. Wednesday 3 June 2009.

Going as far back as the London Transport era, the bus department has always had its own towing service vehicles for when buses broke down on the roadside. Like with many things today, even this was privatised and outsourced to an outside company which means operators having to pay a hefty bill each time their vehicle breaks down and needs a tow. Sovereign are the choice of recovery and are very experienced in fixing buses, sometimes preventing it having to be towed by fixing the fault at the roadside and the bus can carry on in service. This Cricklewood TP has disgraced itself on the 139 and has had to be towed back into the yard approaching its garage on the Edgware Road. Saturday 19 September 2009.

With the delivery of new electric vehicles for the 507 and 521 routes, the released MECs took up service on the 108 replacing some older vehicles on that route, with a small number taking up driver training duties painted into this livery, replacing some of the ageing early PVLs. MEC28 is seen in Greenwich with a novice driver at the wheel. Thursday 5 April 2018. (*Jimmy Sheng*)

London Buses have an Incident Response Unit who are responsible for inspecting and to maintain the roadside infrastructure such as bus stops and bus stations, attending Road Traffic Accidents that a bus may be involved in, or likely to be disrupted from, applying diversion boards to the necessary posts so that drivers know where to divert to, although they do not clean the bus stops; this is sourced to an outside contractor. 7845M is seen in Richmond where its driver had just removed the hood indicating that the bus stop is closed, as well as the special posters indicating this in the timetable frames. Friday 4 January 2019.

London's first dial a ride service was introduced in 1974 in a circular route starting and finishing at Golders Green serving Hampstead Garden Suburbs Monday to Saturday only, but unusually for dial a ride service the route had fixed stops. This lasted until 1976, when it was replaced by route H2. Today's Dial a Ride is a bit different from the original route in that it is not a fixed route, the passenger dials and requests it to pick them up at their home. This service was introduced in 1982 using a single vehicle but today has six bases across the different boroughs of London and has a large fleet of wheelchair accessible buses. For a time, Mercedes Benz Sprinter minibuses were used but new VW T5 Bluebird low floor minibuses have been rolled out network wide. MX68 COJ is one such vehicle seen passing Ealing Common. Saturday 20 April 2019.

Chapter 13

Rail Replacement and Special Bus Services

In 2008, route 51 was newly in the hands of Stagecoach and allocated to Plumstead Garage. Some of Stagecoach's enthusiastic managers and staff arranged to run a Routemaster on the route using RM1941 (BW) borrowed from Bow Garage. It is a very long way off its usual routing between Tower Hill and Trafalgar Square at the Orpington Station terminus where it made a few trips between Woolwich and Orpington. Behind it is another stranger from the east in the form of West Ham Garages 17748 (WH) which has been loaned over until the routes new Scanias arrived. Saturday 6 December 2008.

The annual Chelsea Flower Show sees Go-Ahead London Commercial Fleet provide the shuttle services between Victoria Station and the event transporting many spectators. RML2472 (NX) has just offloaded its passengers and passes some of the Queen's Soldiers collecting for a charity in Royal Hospital Road. Some nice proper blinds have been produced too instead of pieces of paper/slip boards that one can sometimes find placed in windows on some services. Wednesday 26 May 2010.

A vehicle type once present on the London bus scene, both single and dual door version, is the Leyland Olympian, many of which had differing manufacturers' bodies. Wiltax Olympian H48 MJN was new to Colchester Borough Transport in 1991 and has a Leyland body. It was in the Wiltax fleet in 2010 whilst seen on Victoria Line rail replacement in Selborne Walk, Walthamstow. July 2010.

To mark 50 years since route 123 was introduced to replace trolleybuses, Arriva arranged a small running day on the route between Wood Green and Ilford using three of its heritage fleet buses in the form of gold RM6, open top RMC1464, and RML901. The RML would be the last back to Wood Green and is seen just offloading passengers from its last trip into Ilford. The building boarded up in a drab looking material in the background used to be the well-known store Harrison Gibson's, which suffered a couple of fires in days gone by. It is still currently being redeveloped in 2019. Saturday 19 June 2010.

RML2760 (WH) was brought out on the 5 road to do a couple of trips between Romford Market and Barking, London Road one Saturday in May, in order to raise money for a selected charity. This day took full advantage of the busy Saturday shoppers who travelled to Barking and Romford to shop. The bus is seen on the bus stand in London Road, Barking. Saturday 14 May 2011.

On Friday 16 September 2011, Upton Park Garage closed its doors for good before it was demolished to make way for a new housing development and all the routes moved over to the new West Ham Garage, except for the 101, which was allocated to Barking. As a tribute and send off to the garage, London Bus Company RT3062 and RT3871 were used on some timetabled journeys throughout the day well into the evening peak over the route. Whilst the crews took a lunch break, both buses are seen standing inside the garage from the Redclyffe Road exit; this garage operated a one-way system with buses entering from Priory Road and exiting from this exit. Friday 16 September 2011.

'The Year Of The Bus' in 2014 brought numerous garage open days and special route workings. An interesting working was an RT on single deck route 100 traversing down the old back streets of Wapping which retains its old East London character, but with many of the former dockside warehouse buildings now being expensive apartments. RT3251 did the honours and is seen at the Elephant & Castle bus stop before it made a non-stop run down the Walworth Road, to Walworth Garage where an open day was organised. Saturday 19 July 2014.

A regular yearly event has taken place in the last couple of years where we have seen Sir Peter Hendy's RM1005 perform on a chosen route, collecting money for the Royal British Legion Poppy Appeal. Here it crosses Waterloo Bridge on the 188 heading for North Greenwich. Somerset House is the background setting for this scene and the original was built for Edward Seymour, Duke of Somerset, in 1547. It was demolished and rebuilt to the house we see today and has had many uses over the years from Naval offices, Taxes, Stamp, and Inland Revenue offices, to an art gallery/exhibition/museum of today. Friday 7 November 2014.

Although LT's fleet gave a whole load of trouble and mechanical issues with some lasting less than ten years in service, or being off the road longer than in service, surprisingly the DMS gave better service to operators outside of London, which does prove that London conditions need buses built for and tailored for its services and traffic conditions. Ensignbus's DMS2646 made an appearance on the route 31 running day which was connected to the garage open day at Westbourne Park, where it is seen a few stops down Western Road. This exact vehicle carried this livery when it and numerous Routemasters received it in 1979 in celebration of 150 years of the London Bus. Saturday 10 October 2015.

A running day was arranged on several routes in Central London on this day. As well as the usual routes such as the 9, 15, and 159, there were some new routes that haven't really been done before, one such working seen turning into the Kennington Road opposite the Imperial War Museum at Kennington Park on a short working as far as Brixton, is RML2760 on the 3. This bus has been given to the London Bus Museum on long term loan from Stagecoach London and looks very nice with yellow adverts for their museum in Brooklands. This bus worked a few trips on route 38 later in the day. Sunday 8 October 2017.

2019 marked 40 years since the last RFs (30 March 1979) on the 218/219, and RTs (7 April 1979) on the 62 operated with London Transport at Kingston and Barking Garages respectively. To celebrate this, Amersham and District Motorbus Society arranged a running day in the Kingston, Staines, and Weybridge area. The 218 and 219 were the main routes, however, other routes included were the 215/215A, 456B, 460, 462, 462B, 725, and the 727 which didn't restrict to using just RF vehicles; an RT, Routemaster, and Leyland National were amongst other vehicles which performed on some of the aforementioned routes. RF486 speeds through the Dittons on a run to Staines. Sunday 24 March 2019.

As with the RFs, 2019 also marked 40 years since the RT was withdrawn from passenger service back on the 7 April 1979 from Barking Garage, with route 62 having the honour of being the last route. A running day was organised over route 62 as well as special runs on old routes 23C, 87, 106, 721, 722, 723, as well as an RF on the old route 291 which was allocated to Barking Garage. As well as the running day, both Barking, and River Road Garages held open days with vehicle displays and trade stalls. RT1702 is a regular performer at events and running days and looks rather resplendent with its well-kept appearance seen in Upney Lane going to Chadwell Heath, which is where a narrow bridge at the station helped the RTs to have an extended life. This running day fell on the exact day 40 years after the last RFs ran at Kingston. Saturday 30 March 2019.

The Wimbledon Tennis fortnight brings droves of spectators to Wimbledon every year from all over the country and abroad. Go-Ahead have provided the service for many years and have used various bus types from their fleet. One vehicle type that has consistently turned up are Routemasters such as RML2604 descending Wimbledon Hill through very serene settings to collect more punters waiting at the station. Friday 12 July 2019.

With the changes to route 140 and the introduction of new routes in the Harrow and Heathrow area, two weeks before the London Bus Museum organised a running day over the full 140 route, along with the odd trips over the 114 using RTs, RMs and two Metrobuses, all of which operated the route over the years. Back in the 1970s, the 140 was going to be London's last RT route but the road bridge in Chadwell Heath on route 62 changed the plans. RM835 was nice to see bringing a touch of colour to Harrow on a dreary wet day in its Clydeside livery. This vehicle was purchased by Clydeside from LT in 1986 in order to compete with other services during deregulation in Glasgow. The livery in comparison is very similar to the brief Shop Linker livery which was worn by some chosen vehicles for the Shop Linker service in Central London in 1979. Saturday 23 November 2019.